BIG BOOK OF
CHRISTMAS
ORNAMENTS AND DECORATIONS

BIG BOOK OF
CHRISTMAS
ORNAMENTS AND DECORATIONS

37 Favorite Projects and Patterns
The Best of *Scroll Saw Woodworking & Crafts* Magazine

From the Editors of
Scroll Saw Woodworking & Crafts

Christmas Angel Wreath,
by Kathy Wise, page 148.

FOX CHAPEL
PUBLISHING

Cover art: *Whimsical Christmas Ornaments* by Kathy Wise, page 72.

© 2011 by Fox Chapel Publishing Company, Inc., East Petersburg, PA.

Patterns on pages 70, 71, 78-81, 85, 146, 147, and 152 are © 2011 by Kathy Wise Designs Inc.

Big Book of Christmas Ornaments and Decorations is an original work, first published in 2011 by Fox Chapel Publishing Company, Inc. The patterns contained herein are copyrighted by the author. Readers may make copies of these patterns for personal use. The patterns themselves, however, are not to be duplicated for resale or distribution under any circumstances. Any such copying is a violation of copyright law.

ISBN 978-1-56523-606-6

Library of Congress Cataloging-in-Publication Data

Big book of Christmas ornaments and decorations / from the editors of Scroll saw woodworking & crafts.

   p. cm. -- (The best of Scroll saw woodworking & crafts magazine)

Includes index.

ISBN 978-1-56523-606-6 (alk. paper)

1. Christmas decorations. 2. Handicraft. 3. Woodwork--Patterns. I. Scroll saw woodworking & crafts magazine.

TT900.C4B546 2011

745.594'12--dc23

       2011014539

To learn more about the other great books from Fox Chapel Publishing, or to find a retailer near you, call toll-free 800-457-9112 or visit us at *www.FoxChapelPublishing.com*.

Note to Authors: We are always looking for talented authors to write new books in our area of woodworking, design, and related crafts. Please send a brief letter describing your idea to Acquisition Editor, 1970 Broad Street, East Petersburg, PA 17520.

Printed in China
First printing: September 2011

tents

What You Can Learn

How to Add Color with Acrylic

How to Make Delicate Compound Cuts

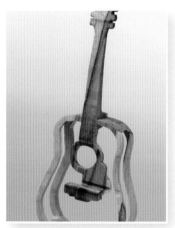

How to Scroll CDs

How to Create Inlay

How to Add a Third Dimension

3-D Snowflake Ornaments, 36

How to Use Scraps

Scrap Wood Snowflakes, 15

12-Piece Intarsia Nativity Set, 66

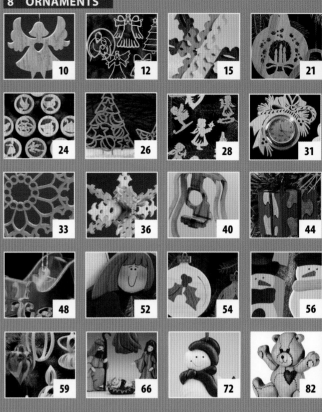

Ornaments

Look no further for ornament inspiration—no matter what the Christmas tree, you're sure to find the perfect adornment somewhere among these projects. There are fancy fretwork designs, touchable intarsia collections, 3-D compound-cut dazzlers, colorful inlaid figures, and even a shiny way to make those used CDs beautiful. Some are easy, some more challenging. Have fun browsing the beautiful, serious, and whimsical options and then making them!

Santa's Workshop Ornaments,
by Kathy Wise, page 82.

Classic Holiday
ORNAMENTS

By John A. Nelson

It's never too early to start cutting Christmas ornaments! Friends and family love getting new ones each year, and stack cutting lets you make a bundle of these festive designs in no time.

The patterns can be reduced or enlarged to fit the wood you have available, making these ornaments a great way to use up scrap pieces of hardwood or Baltic birch plywood. To add contrast, stack a piece of colored acrylic to the star or stocking when cutting the outer perimeter. Attach the acrylic to the back of the ornament and position in front of a light for a warm glow.

materials & tools

MATERIALS:
- Assorted scraps ⅛" to ¼" thick and up to 5" x 5"
- Finish of choice (I use a spray lacquer)

TOOLS:
- #1 and #5 reverse-tooth blades or blades of choice
- Sandpaper, 220-grit

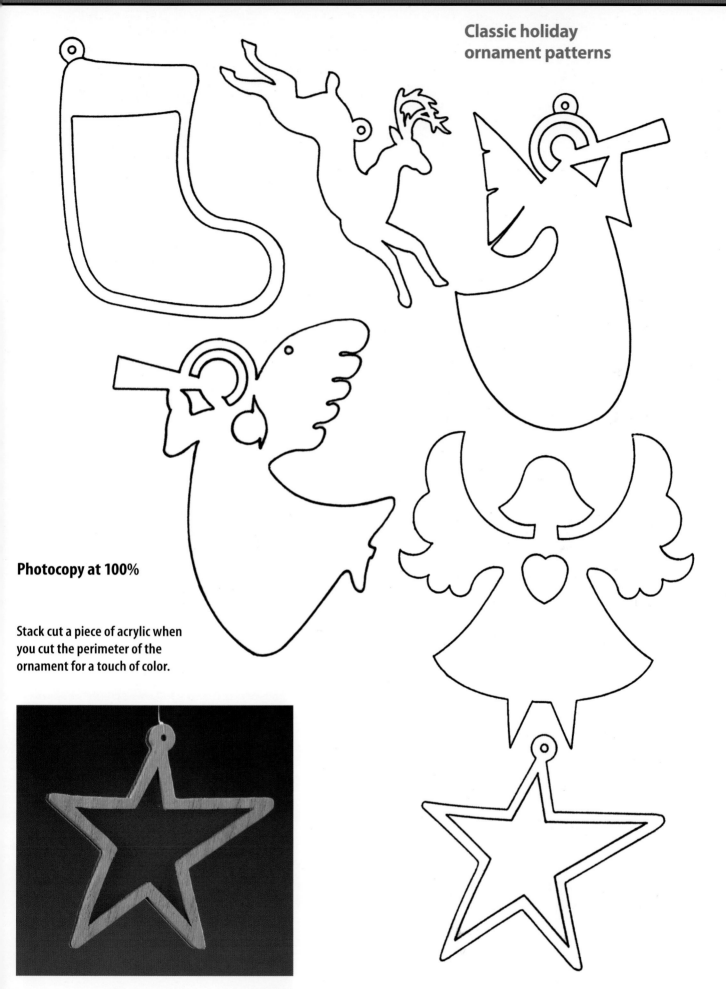

Photocopy at 100%

Stack cut a piece of acrylic when you cut the perimeter of the ornament for a touch of color.

Delicate Christmas Ornaments

By Tom Zieg

These fresh, new designs are perfect for everyone on your Christmas list. These patterns are fairly simple and easy to scroll.

Like most of my ornament designs, these six patterns are designed to be cut from ⅛"-thick Baltic birch plywood. The layered composition of the plywood supports the delicate designs.

You can cut them from hardwood, but be careful when positioning the pattern in relation to the grain. Hardwood ornaments are much more durable if you increase the size of the patterns by photocopying them at 150%.

Because the pieces are very delicate, I usually stack cut them in sets of four or five. Not only do the extra layers support the delicate fretwork, but it is easier to cut the thicker stack. Thin wood is difficult to cut accurately on a scroll saw.

Use caution when sanding the delicate ornaments. It is easy to snap them! I recommend placing your sandpaper on a flat surface and sliding the ornament over the sandpaper.

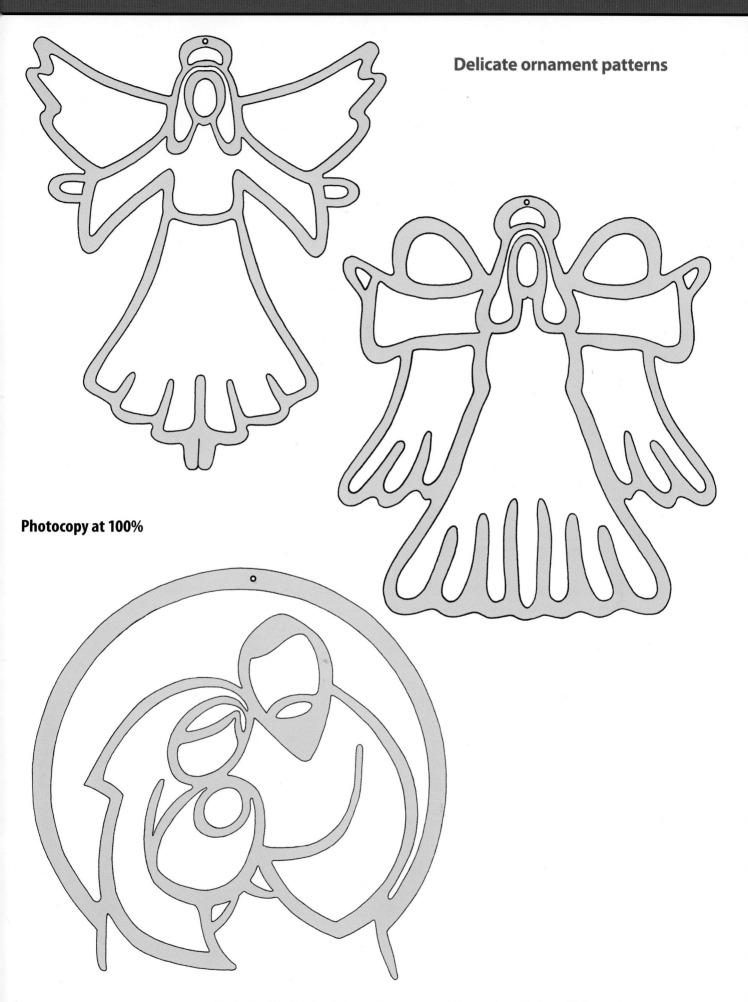

Delicate ornament patterns

Photocopy at 100%

Delicate ornament patterns

materials
& tools

MATERIALS:
- ⅛" x 5" x 5" Baltic birch plywood or wood of choice (per ornament)
- Sandpaper, 220-grit
- Finish of choice

TOOLS:
- #1 reverse-tooth blades or blades of choice
- Drill with assorted small drill bits

Scrap Wood Snowflakes

By Gary MacKay

This scrap wood pile represents nearly a dozen species of wood. It made 69 snowflakes.

I was looking for a way to use the pile of scrap wood that continually accumulates in my shop. With the holidays right around the corner, I designed these snowflakes specifically to use that pile and provide a way to replenish my wood supply.

My only criteria in saving a piece of wood is it must be at least ¼" thick. I sell the snowflakes that I make at craft galleries, and they go a long way to paying for my next trip to the hardwood store. I can then buy hardwood for my larger projects and make more scrap wood to inspire new smaller designs.

Water makes a six-sided crystal when frozen, so all of these snowflake patterns have six arms. You need only your scroll saw and two pieces of contrasting wood that measure ¼" x 5½" x 5½" to make two pie-shaped laminations and two snowflakes where every other arm is contrasting wood.

Because I don't really need to worry about structural strength, I glue the scrap pieces end to end to give me a piece long enough for the snowflake pattern. Cut these pieces into strips of varying widths from ½" to 2". Glue the strips together, alternating contrasting woods, to get a piece wide enough for your pattern. Plane or sand it down to ¼"-thick.

Straight edge laminations

You will need to make a gluing jig if you are making straight edge laminations. (See the gluing jig diagram on page 18, and glue the fence onto the base.) Put old newspaper on top of the jig to catch any extra glue.

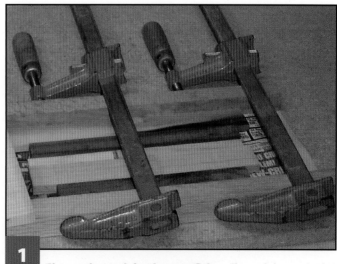

1

Glue up the stock for the snowflakes. Glue and clamp mixed stock into sheets that are 5" wide and 5½" long or multiples of 5½" long. Plane or sand your stock to the proper thickness.

2 **Cut out the snowflakes.** You can stack cut two or more layers together. Transfer the pattern to the blank. Drill blade-entry holes and the hanging hole with a ¹⁄₁₆"-diameter drill bit. Cut the frets first with a #5 reverse-tooth blade. Then cut the profile of the snowflakes.

3 **Cut the pie-shaped pieces for lamination.** Use three strips of double-sided tape to adhere one light-colored blank to one dark-colored blank. Transfer the pattern onto the stack. Cut the segments. Drive a putty knife between the two blanks with a hammer to separate the stack.

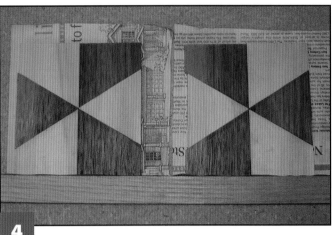

4 **Glue up the six segments.** Separate the segments into two pie-shaped blanks, alternating light and dark woods. Return the segments to their originally cut positions, with segment 1 next to segment 2 and so forth. Glue up both blanks on a sheet of old newspaper. Sand both sides of the segment blank to remove any dried glue or newspaper.

5 **Transfer the snowflake pattern to the blank.** It is difficult to align two pie-shaped blanks together, so I don't stack cut them. Spray adhesive onto the back of the pattern. Push a pin through the center of the pattern into the center of the laminated blank. Slide the pattern down the pin, aligning the six lines of the pattern with the six joints.

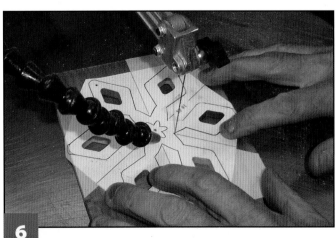

6 **Cut out the snowflake.** Drill blade-entry holes for the frets with a ¹⁄₁₆"-diameter drill bit. Cut the inside frets first with a #5 reverse-tooth blade. Then cut the perimeter of the snowflake.

7 **Apply your finish of choice.** Sand away any fuzzies with 220-grit sandpaper. Dip the snowflakes in tung oil poured into an aluminum baking pan that has a corner crimped into a "V". Wipe them dry with lint-free rags. Pour the tung oil back into the can when done. Hang the used rags outside to thoroughly dry before disposing of them.

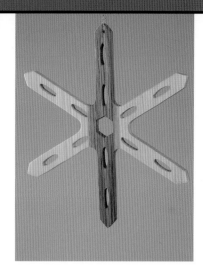
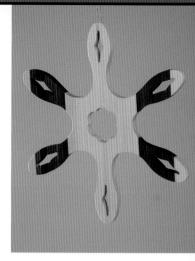

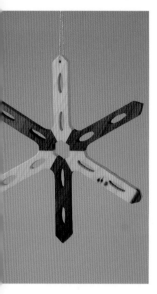
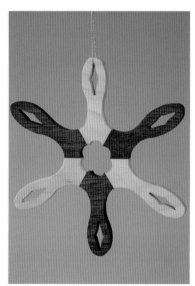

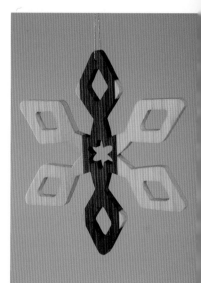

PLANING GLUE-UPS

tips

Do not plane wood that has been glued end grain-to-end grain, as it may break in your planer. You need to cut this wood into strips, and edge-glue it to other strips, offsetting the end grain laminations, before running it through the planer.

MATERIALS:

- ¾" x 18" x 24" medium density fiberboard (MDF) (gluing-jig base)
- ¾" x ¾" x 24" any wood species (gluing-jig fence)
- 10 each ¼" x ½" x 5½" scrap contrasting wood (straight laminations)
- ¼" x 5½" x 5½" light colored wood (pie-shaped laminations)
- ¼" x 5½" x 5½" dark colored wood (pie-shaped laminations)
- Wood glue
- Temporary-bond spray adhesive
- Clear packaging tape (to stack cut)
- Old newspaper
- String or fishing line (for hanging snowflake ornaments)
- 2 each scrap wood clamping blocks
- Double-sided tape or hot melt glue gun
- Assorted grits of sandpaper

TOOLS:

- Table saw, planer, band saw optional (for machining scrap wood prior to gluing)
- #5 reverse-tooth blade or blades of choice
- Putty knife
- Hammer
- Razor blade holder with razor blade (to scrape off dried glue, newspaper)
- 2 screw-type clamps
- A palm, orbital, or belt sander

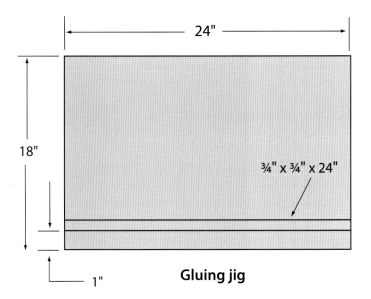

Pie-shaped lamination pattern

Photocopy at 100%

¾" x ¾" x 24"

24"

18"

1"

Gluing jig

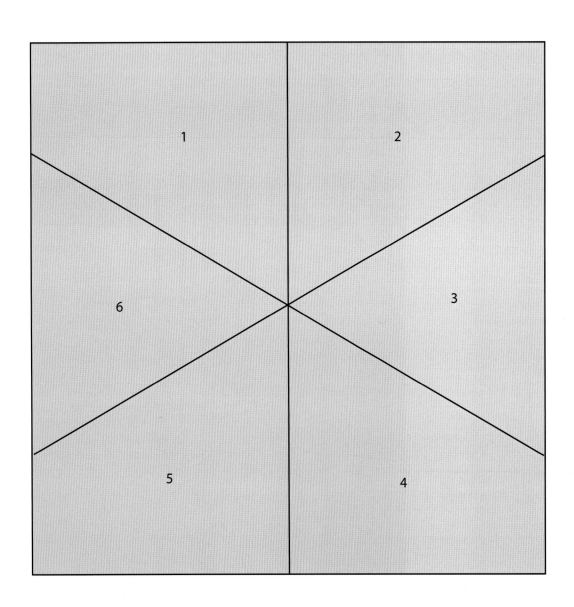

Scrap wood ornament
patterns

Photocopy at 100%

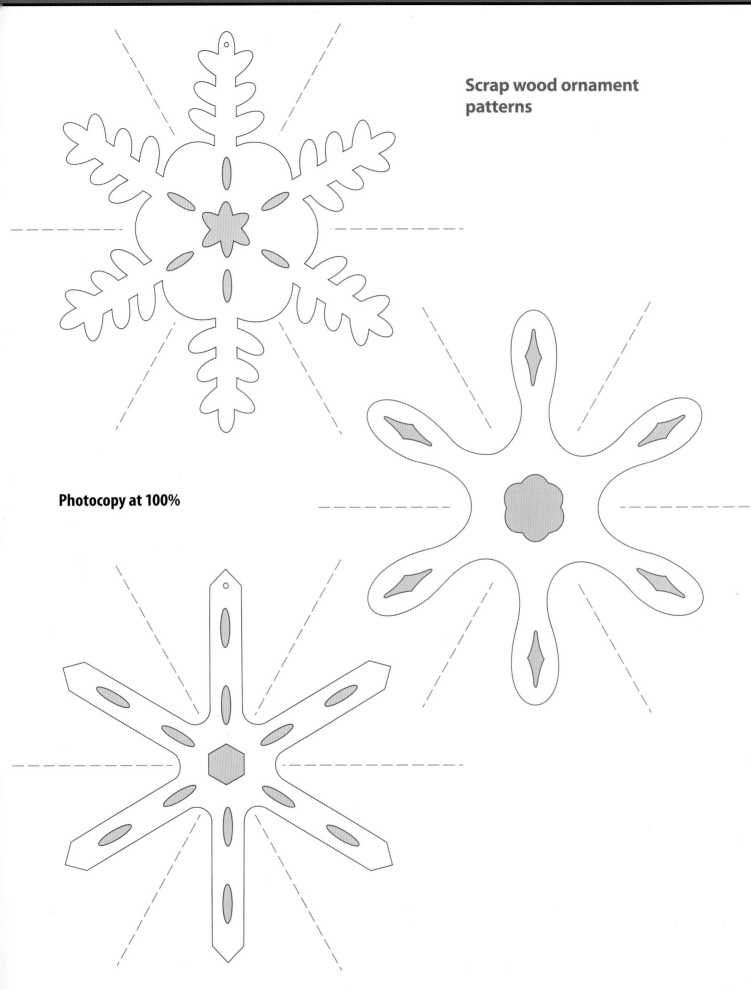

Scrap wood ornament patterns

Photocopy at 100%

Classic Patterns for Holiday Ornaments

Versatile designs can be used several ways.

By Paul Meisel

The seven classic holiday designs shown here can each be made in three different styles.

For traditional ornaments, hang each with a loop of ribbon.

For refrigerator adornments, leave the top tab solid and use epoxy adhesive to mount a magnet on the back.

For small wind chimes, drill five ³⁄₃₂"-diameter holes as shown and tie on the chimes with separate pieces of string.

I recommend cutting the projects from ¼"-thick hardwood or red oak plywood. Attach a photocopy of the pattern to the wood with spray adhesive. Drill blade-entry holes and cut the fretwork. Don't drill the five holes at the bottom if you're not making wind chimes. Then cut around the perimeter of the designs.

Drill a ⅛"-diameter hole or cut the opening in the top if you will be hanging the project. Because these cutouts are rather intricate, I use a can of clear polyurethane aerosol spray to finish them.

Classic ornament patterns

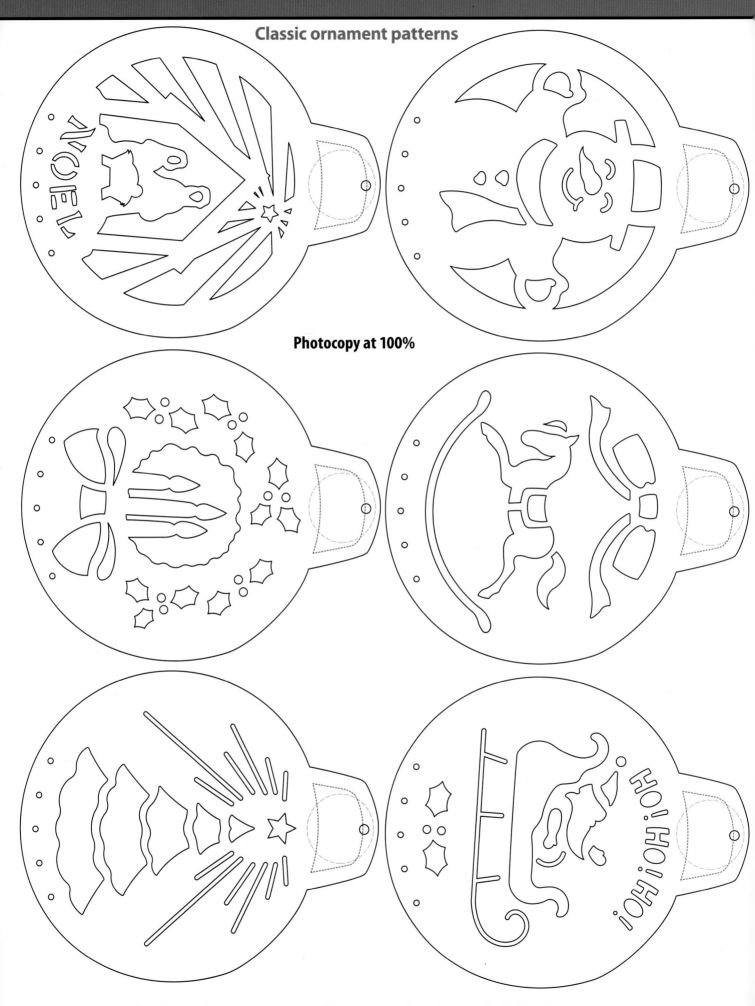

Photocopy at 100%

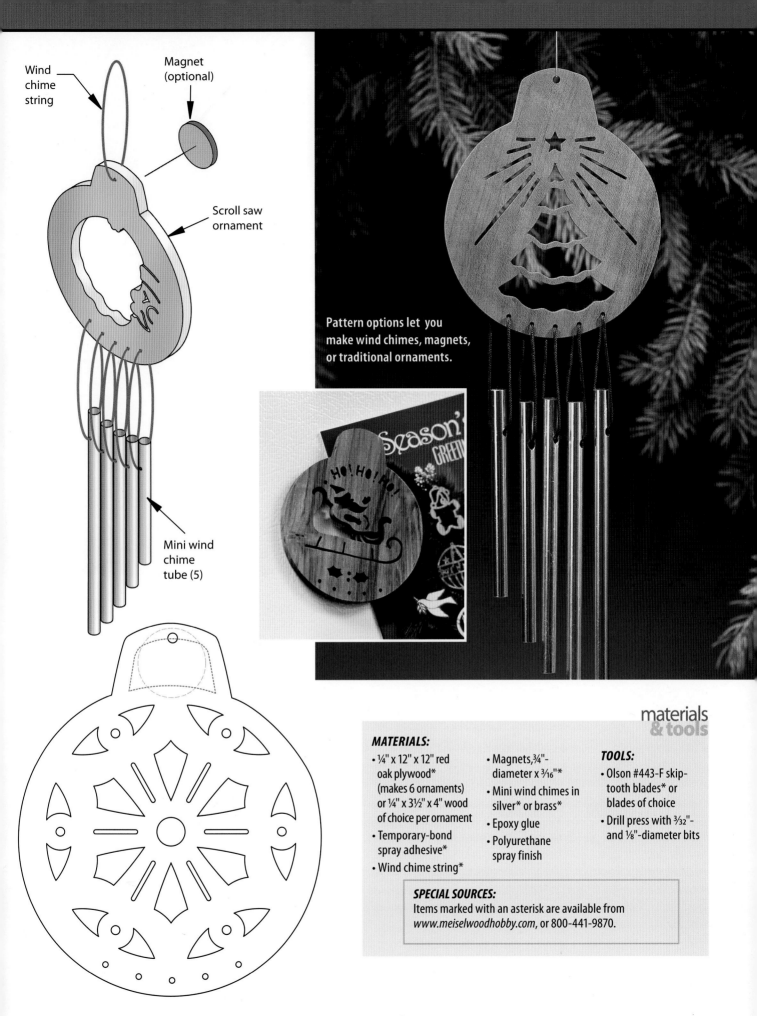

Wind chime string

Magnet (optional)

Scroll saw ornament

Mini wind chime tube (5)

Pattern options let you make wind chimes, magnets, or traditional ornaments.

12 Days of Christmas Ornaments

By Sue Mey

Easy to stack cut, these ornaments help spread holiday cheer

These ornaments depict the objects in the popular song "The Twelve Days of Christmas."

Sand the plywood, and use double-sided tape to prepare them for stack-cutting. Attach the patterns to the plywood stack. Use a ⅛"-diameter bit to drill blade-entry holes and the hanging hole at the top of each pattern. Use a ⅟₃₂"-diameter bit to drill eye holes where indicated.

Carefully remove the burrs created by drilling the holes, using a scraper blade or utility knife. Make the large inside cuts using a #2 reverse-tooth blade. Slow down the speed of the scroll saw and be very careful when you make the fine inside cuts using a #2/0 blade. Remove the waste pieces. Cut in the veining details and reverse carefully out of the cuts.

Cut the blank into separate ornaments, using a #5 or #7 reverse-tooth blade or your blade of choice. Add the correct number of medium-density fiberboard backing pieces to each ornament's stack, then cut around the outside pattern line. Sand the edges. Separate the wood layers, keeping track of the backers that go with each stack. Remove the patterns and use extreme care and 150-grit sandpaper to sand the ornaments. Remove the dust and use a brush to apply the finish to the plywood. Allow the ornaments to dry thoroughly.

Apply several light coats of spray paint to the backer boards, adding splashes of contrasting color when it is dry, if you wish. Glue the ornaments and backer board together, and finish with clear spray varnish.

material & tool

MATERIALS:
- ⅛" x 2 ¾" x 2 ⅜" plywood (for each ornament)
- ⅛" x 2 ¾" x 2 ⅜" MDF (for each ornament)
- Temporary-bond spray adhesive
- Thin, double-sided tape
- Masking tape
- Wood glue
- Spray paints in colors of choice
- Deep penetrating furniture wax liquid or Danish oil
- Clear spray varnish
- Gold string or thin, colored ribbon

TOOLS:
- #2, #2/0, and #5 or #7 reverse-tooth blades or blades of choice
- Drill press with ⅛", ⅟₁₆" and ⅟₃₂"-diameter drill bits
- Sandpaper, assorted grits
- Disc sander and palm sander
- Scraper blade or utility knife blade
- Artist's brush
- Small clamps

Photocopy at 100%

Fretwork Christmas Ornaments

By John A. Nelson

Christmas ornaments make great gifts for family members. They're easy to stack cut so you can make enough to fill everyone's stocking in no time. Tuck one into your holiday cards or attach them to a gift for a special presentation.

Reduce or enlarge the patterns as you wish—these ornaments are a great way to use scrap pieces of hardwood or Baltic birch plywood.

The ornaments can be cut from hardwood, colored acrylic, or plywood. Try painting the plywood version with festive colors or stack cutting a piece of acrylic when making the perimeter cut for a stained glass effect.

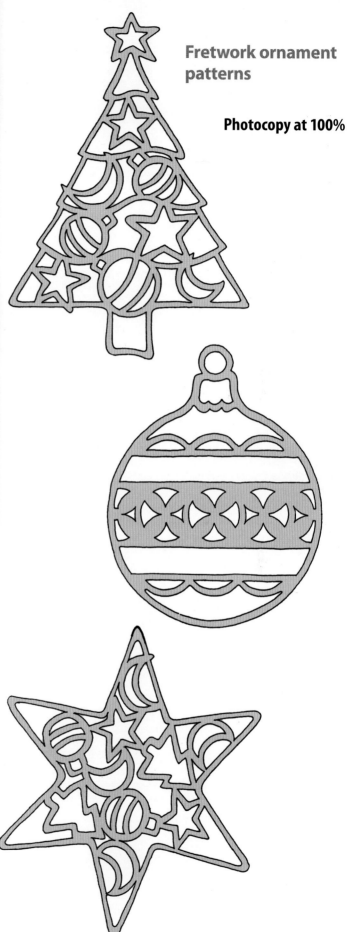

Fretwork ornament patterns

Photocopy at 100%

materials & tools

MATERIALS:
- Assorted scraps ⅛" to ¼" thick and up to 5" x 5"
- Finish of choice (I use a spray lacquer)

TOOLS:
- #1 and #5 reverse-tooth blades or blades of choice
- Sandpaper, 220-grit

European Fretwork Ornaments

By Tom Sevy

Design by Volker Arnold

These classic German ornaments lend an air of nostalgia to your Christmas tree. You can also slip one in the envelope before mailing your Christmas cards or use them to dress up a wrapped gift. The slotted trees can be used as ornaments or enlarged for use as a centerpiece for your holiday dinner. Attach the trees to a circular base for stability if you want them to stand on their own.

Reduce or enlarge the patterns to suit your needs. Use standard stack-cutting techniques to speed production. If you cut the ornaments individually, avoid using a reverse-tooth blade; the reversed teeth at the bottom will cut up through the thin wood and create fuzzies on the top.

I cut the veining lines with a small spiral blade to make them more prominent. Alternatively, you can burn the lines with a woodburner. Clean up the cuts with needle files or strips of sandpaper.

Traditionally, German ornaments are cut from plywood and not sealed or finished. You can cut the designs from hardwood or apply acrylic paints for a more festive look. I recommend using a spray lacquer or varnish to protect the wood.

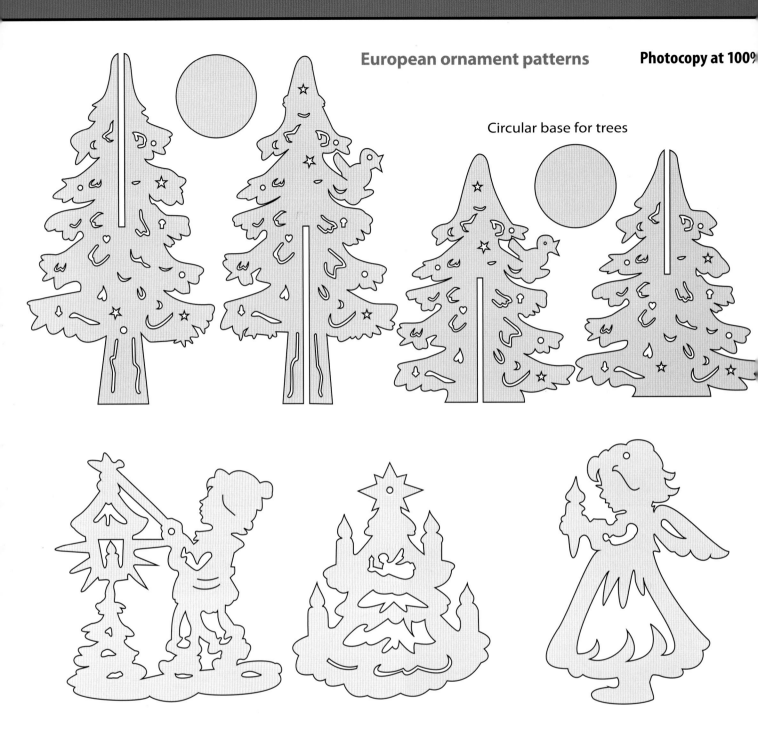

European ornament patterns

Photocopy at 100%

Circular base for trees

Ribbon Ornaments

By Lora S. Irish

These simple designs add elegance to classic sentiments of the season. Add a ribbon and you can also use them to adorn holiday gifts.

Step 1: Copy the pattern, and attach it to the wood, using your method of choice.

Step 2: Drill blade-entry holes for the interior cuts. For the detail cuts in the interior plate, use a drill bit just large enough to feed the #3 blade, or your blade of choice, through.

Step 3: Cut the inside fretwork with the #3 blade or your blade of choice. Start in the center, and work your way out. Do the more delicate areas first.

Step 4: Cut the outline or perimeter using a #5 blade or your blade of choice.

Step 5: Sand off any rough edges or burrs from the cutting.

Step 6: Apply your finish of choice. After the finish dries, spray the entire project with clear lacquer.

A few minor alterations create many possibilities

- Enlarge the pattern and add a base for a tealight candle
- Make a clock by adding an inexpensive insert to the "O"
- Use the "O" as a picture frame
- Add a name for distinctive gift tags

materials
& tools

MATERIALS:
- ¼" x 4" x 6" hardwood or plywood of choice
- Spray adhesive or graphite paper (to transfer the pattern)
- Assorted grits of sandpaper
- Finish of choice
- Clear lacquer of choice

TOOLS:
- #3 and #5 scroll saw blades or blades of choice
- Drill
- Assorted small drill bits

Quatre Foils: Based on two common Gothic designs, the pointed arch and quatrefoil (a circle divided into four smaller circles).

Rose Window Ornaments

By Bradford Needham

These ornaments, inspired by the stained-glass windows of the great Cathedrals of Europe, are sure to become treasured keepsakes. They are easily stack cut, enabling you to make enough ornaments to share with family and friends while keeping a set for yourself.

In the twelfth century, knights from Europe brought Greek and Arabic mathematics texts back from the Middle East. These books described the beautiful and subtle geometry of Euclid, which had not been seen in Europe since the fall of the Roman Empire. Using this new geometry, medieval architects designed the soaring Gothic cathedrals, complete with spectacular stained-glass rose windows.

I created these ornament designs using the same methods as the medieval architects: the geometry of Euclid, based on the compass and straightedge (dividers and a ruler). More recently, I've used the computer software *Geometer's Sketchpad* to create these rose-window-inspired designs more quickly and accurately than I can by sketching by hand— still using the same rules developed in ancient Greece and used in medieval Europe.

Six Crowns: A simple design with points similar to crowns.

Chartres: Inspired by the Chartres Cathedral in France.

Star in Clouds: Common design with a circle divided into 12.

Bighorn Flock: Three bighorn sheep gathered around a star.

Rose window ornament patterns

Photocopy at 100%

In making these ornaments, I've experimented with a variety of woods. I enjoy the deep red of cherry and the chocolate brown of walnut. I also like how the light tan of boxwood contrasts nicely with the dark green of a Christmas tree. Experiment yourself, and find the woods you enjoy most.

I suggest cutting the interior spaces in order of size. Start with the smallest holes first and progress to the larger ones. This method retains the strength of the piece as long as possible. Finish by cutting the perimeter of the ornament and lightly sanding to remove any rough edges or adhesive. Apply your finish of choice and hang the ornaments in a well-ventilated area to dry.

If you plan to give the ornaments as a gift, take a moment to include a card stating the year the ornament was crafted, the name of the recipient, and your name as the artisan who crafted the piece. Package the ornament in a small box with some festive tissue paper for a dynamic presentation.

Rose window ornament patterns

Photocopy at 100%

materials & tools

MATERIALS:
- ¼" to ⅜" x 5" x 5" wood of choice (per ornament)
- Glue stick
- Sandpaper, 150 grit
- Clear acrylic finish spray

TOOLS:
- #5 skip-tooth blades or blades of choice
- Drill with ¹⁄₁₆"-diameter drill bit

3-D Snowflake Ornaments

by John A. Nelson

These three-dimensional snowflakes can be stack cut to speed production, and provide an interesting alternative to the traditional flat ornaments.

One word of caution about these patterns; the slots are sized for ⅛"-thick wood. If you buy hardwood or resaw your own wood, you can use the patterns as they are printed. But if you use plywood, check the thickness because not all plywood is the same thickness. Match the width of the slots to the material you are using. These slots should fit tightly for the best results. Position a piece of scrap wood, the same thickness as the wood you plan to use, over the slots in the pattern. Mark a line on both sides of the scrap with a fine mechanical pencil; this lets you tailor the pattern to the exact thickness of your stock.

Drill any blade-entry holes and cut the interior frets before cutting the perimeter of the pattern. Use care when cutting the slots and keep them as straight as possible so the sections of the snowflake fit together properly. If you are not confident in your cutting abilities, cut inside the lines and sand up to the lines with folded sandpaper or small sanding sticks.

Sand both sides of each section and apply your paint or finish of choice. Keep the finish out of the slots. When dry, apply a small amount of glue to the slots, and slide the sections together, following the notations on the pattern. I suggest cyanoacrylate glue. Remove excess glue with cotton swabs. Attach a hanger to complete the ornament.

3-D ornament patterns

Photocopy at 100%

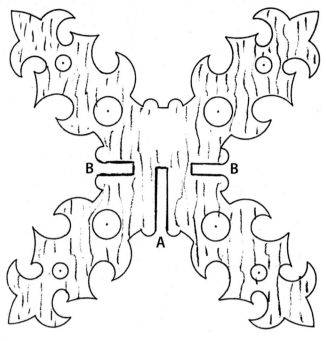

Material thickness

MATERIALS:
- 3 each ⅛" x 4½" x 4½" wood of choice (per ornament)
- Fine mechanical pencil
- Glue of choice
- Assorted grits of sandpaper
- Finish or paint of choice

TOOLS:
- #1 and #3 reverse-tooth blades or blades of choice
- Sanding sticks (optional)

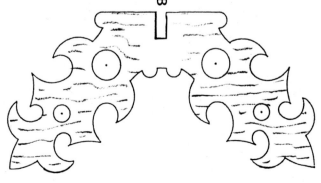

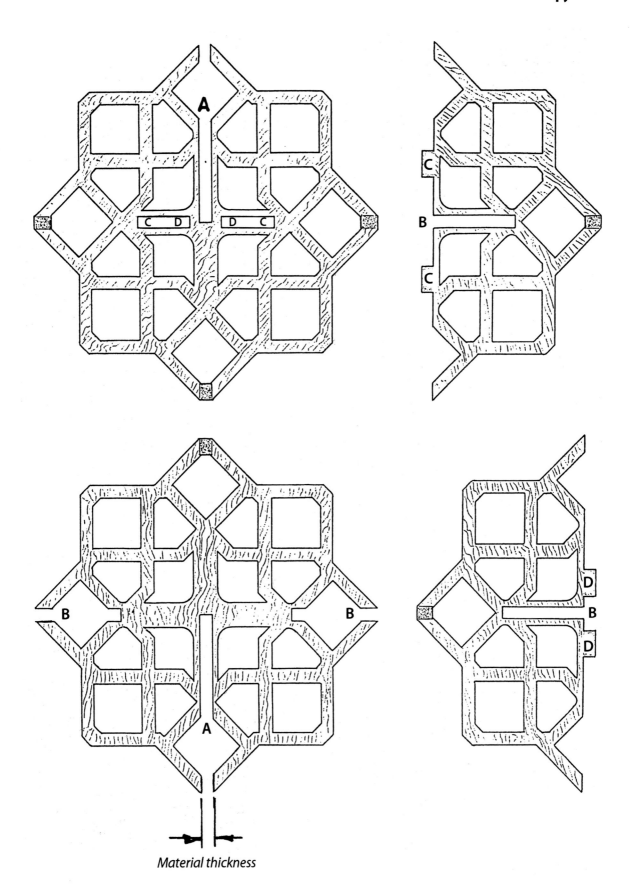

Material thickness

Material thickness

Compound
Musical
Instrument
Ornaments

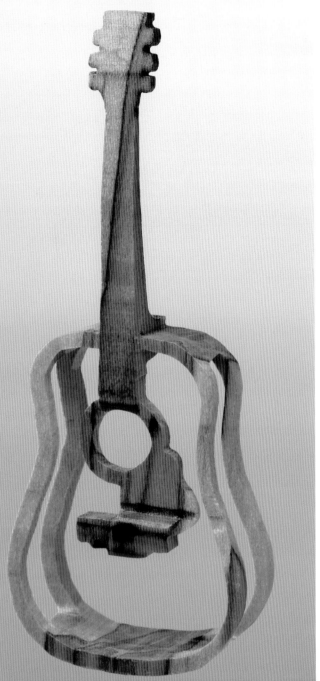

By Stephen Miklos

Compound cutting creates a beautifully intricate design that will be a great conversation piece and a welcome holiday gift.

The finished ornaments are elegant but about as fragile as a glass ornament of similar design. I provide a sturdy gift box filled with wood excelsior (wood shavings used for packing) for storage when they are not on display.

I first became aware of the potential of delicate compound-cut scroll sawing when I saw some geometric ornaments at a craft table in a farmer's market. I hurried home and burned a lot of wood learning to cut thin outlines in thick wood!

I make musical instruments, so I applied the technique to an ornament representing a mountain dulcimer and then a guitar. Not every stringed instrument lends itself to this particular style of design, but my first two ideas worked out.

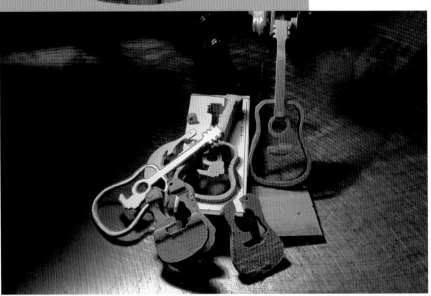

COUNTERING CURLY CHIPS **tips**

Inevitably, when trimming your ornaments, you will get small fringes or curly chips. I attack these with emery boards that I have cut into narrow strips on my scroll saw.

Step 1: Prepare the blank. Cut the wood to the proper dimensions, and make sure the edges are square and true. Fold the pattern on the line shown, and attach it with the fold running along an edge of the blank.

Step 2: Drill blade-entry holes where indicated, using a ⅛"-diameter bit. There's no need to use a tiny drill bit; the ⅛"-diameter bit will easily fit, and it makes threading the blade easier. Be very careful to drill straight through, especially when drilling into the sides. Use a drill press if you can.

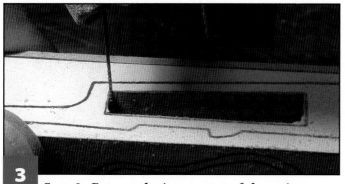

Step 3: Cut out the inner part of the guitar body. All the inside of this cut is waste, so feel free to cut a curve at each corner, cleaning the corners up

Cutting delicate compound patterns

Successfully cutting these designs requires that perpendicular cuts meet with great precision near the middle or bottom of the piece—far from where the blade enters the pattern line.

Keep the blade square to the table and well-tensioned: any blade bowing or deviation in the squareness of the blade to the table can make the strip inelegantly thick or make it disappear when the final cuts are made. Use an aggressive blade, and let it do the work. Don't push too hard against it—that can bow the blade.

Follow the cutting sequence numbered on the pattern to avoid having to tape things back together when moving from cutting the side to cutting the front. The sequence also keeps the piece firmly in the blank until the very last cut, supporting the delicate pieces during the process.

Good woods to use for this kind of project are dense enough to be strong in thin pieces, but soft enough to allow cutting through a thick piece. Mahogany is great because it cuts easily, and the contrasting small pores show up well on the narrow parts of the object. For mahogany or harder woods I do the thick cuts through the width of the block with a #5 skip-tooth blade, and switch to the crown-tooth for the cuts through the face. I use the crown-tooth to prevent chip-out and fraying on the underside of the inner edges of the guitar; a reverse-tooth blade helps with this only at or near the bottom surface. I regularly use soft maple and walnut—but walnut takes an extra long time! For softer woods such as butternut or pine, I use a #5 crown-tooth blade for the whole project.

after removing the waste piece. If the resulting block doesn't slide out easily from both the top and bottom of the hole, check the squareness of the table to the blade before continuing. All cuts from the side require minimum pressure and maximum patience.

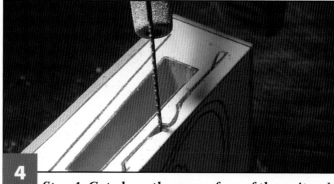

Step 4: Cut along the upper face of the guitar. Use the waste on the upper side to make your sharp corners where the fret board ends and at the front of the bridge.

Step 5: Cut the underside of the guitar. This cut doesn't connect to the previous cut. The cuts from the face side will release the top and bottom ends of the guitar from the block.

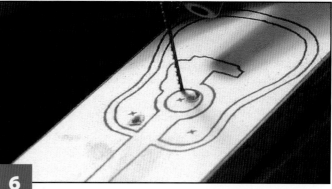

Step 6: Cut out the sound hole. Lay the block flat, thread the blade through the hole in the middle of the sound hole, and cut out this circle.

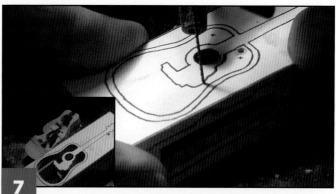

Step 7: Cut around the outside of the sound hole, pick guard, and bridge. Continue around the inner outline of the body. This cut will release three rather interesting pieces of waste.

8 **Step 8: Cut around the outline of the guitar.** Use the waste around the peg head and shoulder to cut from different directions to define the corner and the curves around the tuning buttons, or use on-the-spot turns to accomplish the same thing.

9 **Step 9: Carefully remove the pieces from the blank.** After the outline has been cut around, the guitar and several waste pieces should come right out of the blank. Making the last cut one continuous sweep around the outline assures that the piece comes smoothly out of the block, even if the blade was not quite square.

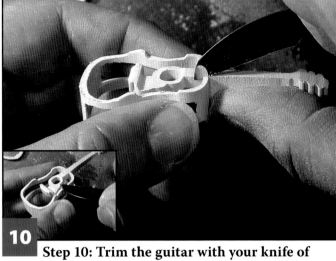

10 **Step 10: Trim the guitar with your knife of choice.** Be sure to hold it by the neck or base; short grain makes the sides extremely fragile. Cutting the contour of the bridge and the fret board leaves humps on the face of the sides that need to be whittled away with a sharp knife. Make a stop cut along the edge of the fret board before trimming the sides in this area.

Step 11: Finish trimming the ornament. Trim the tuning buttons down to make them stand back from the face of the peg head. Then trim off the copy of the sound hole, fret board, and pick guard inside the outline of the back of the guitar. I trim this off with a knife or chisel.

Step 12: Finish your ornament, using your method of choice. I find that spraying a clear finish like shellac or lacquer is easiest. I use glossy spray lacquer. If you use a light-colored wood like pine or poplar, you can dye the wood by dipping it in an aniline dye before spraying. I find the ornament is too delicate and complex to use any rubbed or brushed finishes.

Cutting a Mountain Dulcimer Ornament

The top and bottom of the block form parts of the top and bottom faces of the finished ornament. Because of this, cuts 3 and 10 through 13 start in from the edge rather than from drilled holes. The thickness of the block should just match the size of the side view in the pattern, ⅝".

Cut 3 starts from the back and follows the outline of the scrollhead up to the indicated point where the direction changes. Cuts 8 and 9 do start from drilled holes, but watch out near the other end of the instrument. These cuts don't meet each other, and should end before the end of the block; make sure they go around the outside and don't follow the dotted lines marked "Trim." Cuts 10, 11 and 12 are made in the side of the blank The blade enters from the face side of the pattern.

You will need to trim two pieces from the front of the ornament. Cut straight down with a sharp knife along the dotted lines marked "Trim," and remove the two curved pieces that come loose. You should also trim the tuning knobs as in the guitar pattern.

materials & tools

MATERIALS:	TOOLS:
• ¾" x 1⅜" x 4-5" wood of choice (guitar)	• #5 crown-tooth blade or blade of choice
• ⅝" x 1⅜" x 4-5" wood of choice (dulcimer)	• #5 skip-tooth blade or blade of choice
• Emery boards	• Sharp knife
• Spray lacquer or finish of choice	

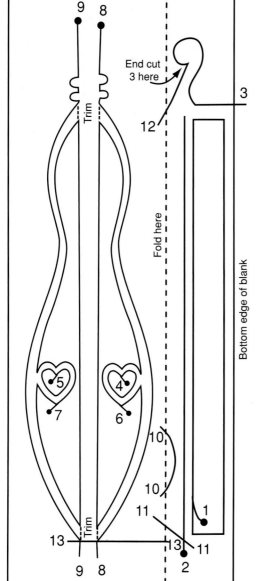

Instrument ornament patterns

Photocopy at 100%

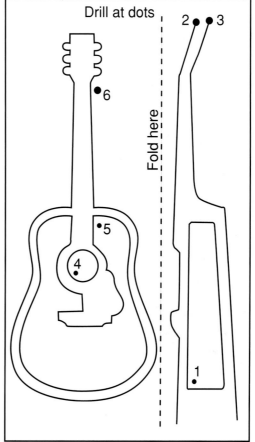

These intricate designs are sure to astound your friends.

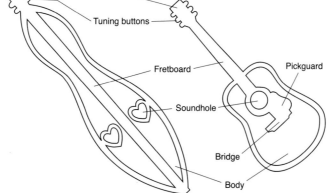

3-D Puzzle Cubes

These puzzle cubes are easy to create, but challenging to reassemble.

By Stephen Miklos

These tiny, compound-cut puzzles look great hanging on a Christmas tree, but also prove fiendishly entertaining as puzzles.

They are simple to make, requiring only one or two cuts per side. Tie a festive ribbon around the assembled puzzle to hold the ornament hook. Once you master the basic technique, you can quickly create a large inventory. They make perfect stocking stuffers or small gifts for friends and colleagues. Because

they are a combination of a puzzle and an ornament, I call them "puzzlements."

Because a 1⅜" cube is difficult to handle under the blade, start by attaching patterns for two or three puzzlements to a 7"-long blank. I use spray adhesive. Make sure the dotted line between the two sides runs straight along the corner of the block. Drill blade-entry holes outside the pattern near the pattern lines at the top and bottom of each side.

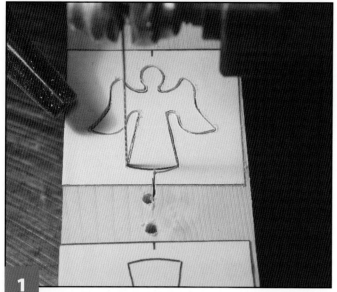

1 **Cut the first outline of the angel.** Use a #5 crown-tooth blade. Start from the blade-entry hole near the bottom of the angel's robe. Make on-the-spot turns at each corner. Stop at the lower corner of the robe, leaving the bottom of the robe uncut. This tab of wood keeps the block intact while you make the cut from the other side, keeping the parts lined up. This tab technique allows a much more precise fit than the tape-in-place method of compound cutting. Rather than backing out of the cut, turn off the saw and release the blade from the blade clamp to remove it from the wood.

2 **Cut the second angel outline.** Start at the blade-entry hole near the hem of the robe. Cut the whole way around the angel shape. The inner figure often jumps up when the cut is complete, and the internal parts have some delicate places, so keep a finger on the angel to prevent breakage. Then turn the block back to the first face, and complete the cut. Feed the blade through the blade-entry hole near the hem, facing away from the cut. Back it up into the cut until it goes around the corner and faces back toward the uncut section. Make the cut. Keep a finger on the angel so it doesn't jump up.

3 **Finish cutting the puzzle.** Insert your blade through the top blade-entry hole. Carefully cut down from the hole to the top of the angel's head. Go very slowly at the end of this cut so you don't nick the angel's head. Cut across the upper and lower edges of the pattern with a #7 precision-ground-tooth (PGT) blade to release the square from the blank.

4 **Take the puzzle apart.** It has to be done in sections. First take away one whole side and then the middle. Then each section can be disassembled. Use caution: many small parts are loose inside the block, and they can become jammed. Work the puzzle back and forth a few times to free them. Discard these small parts; you will reassemble only the nine big parts. To put it back together, assemble the three sections, then slide them together as shown. Use the grain lines to aid in assembly.

5 **Apply the finish.** Sand each face. Be sure to remove any adhesive left behind from the pattern. Mix aniline dyes with water according to the package instructions. Dip the pieces in the dye, then place them on a paper towel to dry. Apply metallic gold spray paint to the face of the angels. Tape the backs to a stick to keep them from blowing away.

6 **Assemble the finished puzzle.** After the finish is dry, assemble the puzzle once more and use a temporary piece of transparent tape on the bottom and top to hold the ornament together while you tie the ribbon. Tie a ribbon or piece of raffia around the square with a bow, and use a standard ornament hook through the ribbon to hang it on the tree.

Alternate Puzzlement Designs

The jigsaw puzzle box is much easier to cut than the angel. Line up three or more patterns on your wood, and start from one of the two blade-entry holes on each face. Cut all the way through the multiple patterns down one side. Using the blade-entry holes instead of entering from the end of the blank creates a tab to keep the pieces intact. Cut both lines, then turn the blank to the other side and make those cuts in the same manner. Cut the squares from the long blank as you did with the angel. Use the patterns given, or lightly draw a pattern freehand with a pencil. The jigsaw designs are very forgiving and do not require precision cutting. I sometimes deviate from a pattern if I think it will improve the piece or make it easier to cut smoothly.

materials & tools

MATERIALS:
- 1⅜" x 1⅜" x 7" soft wood of choice (to make several puzzlements)
- Spray adhesive
- Aniline dye
- Gold spray paint
- Ribbon of choice
- Transparent tape
- Assorted sandpaper up to 220-grit
- Ornament hooks

TOOLS:
- #5 crown-tooth blades or blades of choice
- #7 precision-ground-tooth blades or blades of choice
- Drill with ⅟₁₆"-diameter drill bit

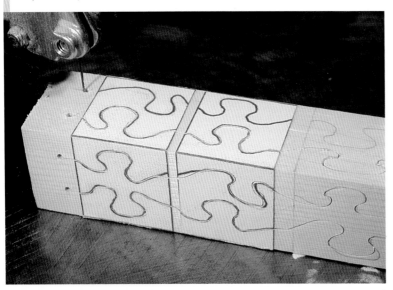

Mix and match the finish colors for a rainbow of ornament options.

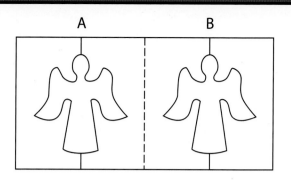

Puzzlement patterns

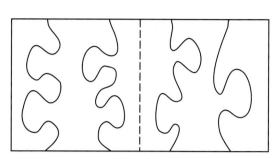

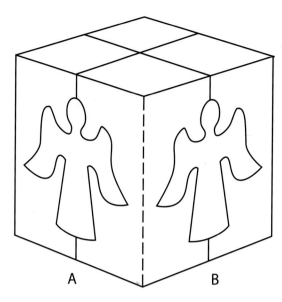

Photocopy at 100%

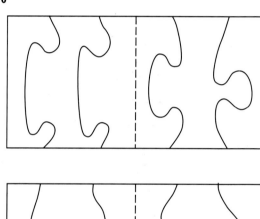

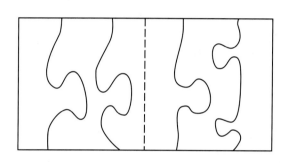

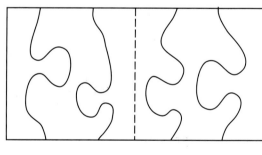

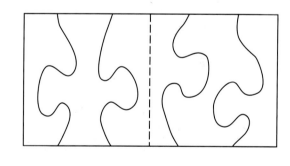

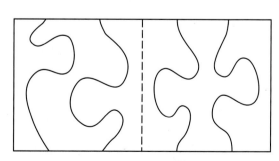

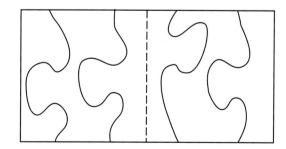

BLADE SELECTION **tips**

I use a #5 crown-tooth blade to cut the puzzlements. It's difficult to cut the thick wood with a finer blade, and a coarser blade leaves too wide of a kerf, making the puzzle loose. I've found a #5 precision-ground-tooth (PGT) blade makes a much bigger kerf than a crown-tooth blade.

Shining Bright

By Carol and Homer Bishop

These ornaments sparkle like diamonds when you light up your Christmas tree. No one will ever know they are made from recycled materials! The slotted designs are easy to cut and assemble and make creative gift tags in addition to being unique ornaments.

The ornaments can be cut from plywood or hardwoods, but the shiny surface of CDs or DVDs gives them an added dimension. The danger of the plastic melting back together is the most difficult part of cutting CDs. Run your saw at a lower speed and use a sharp skip-tooth blade to minimize melting.

1 **Prepare the CD blanks.** Apply spray adhesive to the backs of both CDs. Press them together on a hard flat surface with the shiny side of both CDs facing out. Tape the CDs to a piece of ¼"-thick lauan plywood. The plywood adds support and prevents splitting. Attach the patterns with spray adhesive. Drill the ⅛"-diameter holes for the hanger and any blade-entry holes.

2 **Cut the pieces.** Use a new #4 skip-tooth blade or your blade of choice. Keep the saw speed slow to prevent the plastic from melting. If you notice the burr on the edges of the cut getting bigger, slow down the saw or install a new blade. Peel off the patterns and tape. Use a fingernail to scrape off small burrs and remove the larger burrs with a hobby knife.

3 **Test fit the ornament pieces.** Wipe off the CDs with a soft rag soaked with mineral spirits to remove any remaining adhesive or fingerprints. Make sure the slotted ornaments slide together easily. Sand the wings of the dove and angel at an angle so they fit together tightly when glued. Coat the back of any fragile pieces with cyanoacrylate (CA) glue.

4 **Glue the ornaments together.** Place a drop of CA glue at the end of the slots on the slotted ornaments and slide the two pieces together. Apply just enough glue to cover the edges of the components of the other ornaments. Do not let the glue squeeze out of the joints. Glue the tapered wings onto the dove and angel. Add a string to the top to complete the ornament.

materials
& tools

MATERIALS:
- Several CDs or DVDs
- ¼" x 5" x 5" lauan plywood per CD (to support CDs)
- Metallic cotton embroidery thread (ornament hangers)
- Spray adhesive
- Cyanoacrylate glue
- Blue painter's tape

TOOLS:
- #4 skip-tooth blades or blades of choice
- Sanders of choice
- Drill press with ⅛"-diameter bit

Shining Bright patterns

Photocopy at 100%

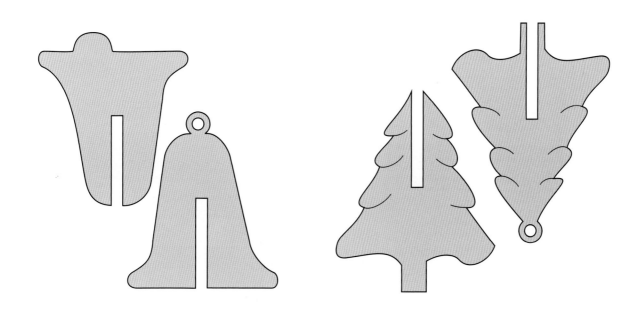

Scroll-and-Paint
Christmas Angel

By Lynn Reno

The holiday season is hectic enough—so a quick and easy angel ornament is just what the doctor ordered to relieve the seasonal stress.

Step 1: Transfer the pattern to the wood. I use temporary bond adhesive, but you can use your method of choice.

Step 2: Cut out the angel pieces. Cut all the pieces using a #3 reverse-tooth blade or your blade of choice. Drill $\frac{5}{64}$"-diameter holes in the edges of the angel's extended hand and the bottom of the star.

Step 3: Sand your angel. I use a flexible-drum sander with a fine sleeve for all my painted woodcrafts. It does a great job of sanding and gets all the fuzzy edges. But the angel is small enough that you can sand it by hand.

Step 4: Basecoat the angel. After removing all the dust from your project, use the flat brush to basecoat the hands, feet, and face with flesh-colored paint. Don't forget to paint the edges, and, for a more finished look, paint the hands and feet on the backside, too. Basecoat both sides of the wings with white. Basecoat the entire star with antique gold. Always keep your brush rinsed. Once the paint has dried, sand very lightly with an extra fine sanding sponge, or a crumpled up brown paper bag, after each coat. Remove the dust and repeat if needed.

Step 5: Shade with a side loaded flat brush. Wet your brush, blot on a paper towel, and dip one corner into slightly diluted shading flesh. Stroke your brush back and forth on a paper plate just like you were painting. This will work the paint into the brush. Dip that corner back into the paint and the other into water. Two strokes on the plate and you should be ready to shade. Practice on a paper plate first and reload your

brush as needed. Keeping the corner with the paint to the outside edge of the face and holding your brush perpendicular to the surface, press the brush to the surface and begin to pull it around the face. If you find the paint has worked it's way to the other end of the brush, rinse it and start over. A damp Q-tip will clean up any ring left in the middle of your piece, if you catch it quickly. Do the same to the hands and feet. Shade the wings by side loading with country tan. Basecoat both sides of the dress with spice red. Shade the dress by side loading with chocolate bar.

Step 6: Paint the head. Dip your scruffy round brush into the spice red and brush it around a fresh paper towel until it is almost all gone. Lightly brush the paint onto your angel's cheeks in a circular motion. If you've never dry brushed cheeks before, you may want to practice on a piece of paper before trying it on your project. Using the graphite paper, lightly trace the hair outline onto the head. If the lines are very dark, partially erase them so you can barely see them. With the round brush, paint the hair and the back of the head golden brown. Add shading to the hair by side-loading the flat brush with nutmeg. Dip the very tip of the round brush into the black paint to add the eyes. Add details and outlines using the pen.

Step 7: Glue the angel and attach the wire. Following the instructions on your adhesive and using the picture as a guide, glue your angel together. With pliers, turn the tip of each end of the wire over and pinch tight. Curl the wire around the $\frac{3}{16}$" piece of dowel. Dip each end into the adhesive and insert one end into the hand and one into the star, using pliers to push them in if needed. Apply finish of choice. I use a clear acrylic spray. Make a hanger for your ornament by folding the jute in half and hot gluing to the back.

MATERIALS:

- ¼" x 4" x 5½" Baltic birch
- Temporary bond spray adhesive
- Acrylic paints:
  Flesh
  Spice red
  Antique gold
  White, country tan
  Chocolate bar
  Golden brown
  Black, and nutmeg brown
  Shading flesh
- Paper towels
- Paper plate
- Micron 01 permanent pen
- 3" 20 gauge annealed wire
- Clear acrylic finish spray
- 9" jute
- Graphite paper

TOOLS:

- #3 reverse tooth scroll saw blades or blades of choice
- Drill with ⁵⁄₆₄"-diameter bit
- Flexible-drum sander with 220-grit sleeve or sander of choice
- ½" flat brush
- Small scruffy round brush
- Small round brush
- Extra fine sanding sponge, or crumpled brown paper bag
- Eraser
- Pliers
- Hot glue gun
- ³⁄₁₆"-diameter dowel

Photocopy at 100%

Inlay Christmas Bulbs

By Theresa Ekdom

Contrasting woods bring these classic symbols of Christmas to life. The traditional bulb shape with hardware overlay design adds a nostalgic flair to the handcrafted hardwood ornaments.

Stack two pieces of scrap wood together and test different angles on your saw table until the inlay fits flush in the base stock. Once you have determined the correct table angle, stack the wood for the inlay design on top of the base wood and attach the pattern to the inlay stock. Cut the inlay, then glue it in place flush with the base wood. When the glue is dry, sand the stock smooth. Return the table to square, cut any veining lines first, then cut the perimeter of the ornament.

The overlays on the top of the bulbs are cut from ¼₆"-thick walnut. Stack several pieces of wood together and wrap masking tape around the stack.

Attach the overlay pattern with spray adhesive and drill ¼₆"-diameter blade-entry holes for the frets. With the table square to the blade, cut the frets with a #1 reverse-tooth blade. Cut along the bottom perimeter line, but cut ⅛" outside the lines along the top and sides. Glue an overlay onto each side of the ornament. Allow the glue to dry, then sand the sides and top flush with the edges of the ornament. Apply tung oil to the completed ornament according to the manufacturer's instructions. Drill two tiny holes in the top of the ornament. Bend the 1"-long piece of fine wire over a 1/8"-diameter dowel to form a "U" shape. Glue the ends of the wire into the two holes with cyanoacrylate (CA) glue.

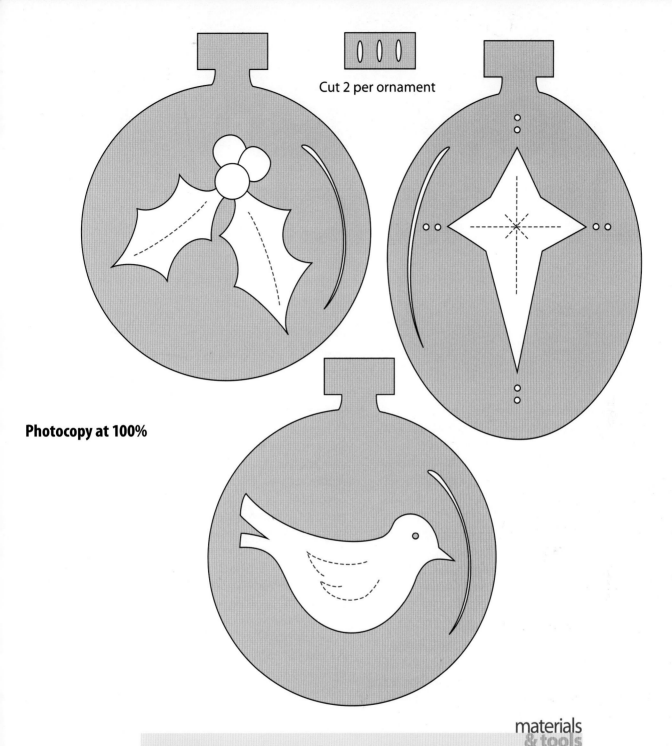

Cut 2 per ornament

Photocopy at 100%

<table>
<tr><td colspan="2">materials
& tools</td></tr>
<tr>
<td>

MATERIALS:
- Assorted ¼"-thick hardwood scraps in various colors
- 2 each ¹⁄₁₆" x ½" x 1" walnut (overlays, per ornament)
- 1"-long piece of 20-gauge wire (per ornament)
- Glue stick or spray adhesive (to attach pattern to wood)
- Wood glue

</td>
<td>

- Cyanoacrylate glue
- Tung oil or finish of choice
- Assorted grits of sandpaper

TOOLS:
- #1 reverse-tooth blades or blade of choice
- Drill with assorted small drill bits
- ⅛"-diameter dowel (to bend wire to shape)

</td>
</tr>
</table>

Making Inlay Snowmen Ornaments

By Theresa Ekdom

Add some color to your holiday tree with these fun and festive inlay ornaments. The whimsical snowman designs are sure to become family favorites. Use the ornaments to decorate a wreath, add a personal touch to wrapped gifts, or tuck them in with your Christmas cards.

The snowmen are a great way to use up small pieces of colorful hardwoods. For these designs, I use padauk, yellowheart, rosewood, purpleheart, zebrawood, and wengé.

Setting the correct table angle

Before cutting the ornaments, determine the correct table angle. Use scrap wood the same thickness as the stock you will be using for the ornaments. Attach two pieces of the testing stock together by running a line of hot glue along their edges. Tilt the right side of the saw table down 2½°. Drill a blade-entry hole with the smallest bit possible. Cut clockwise around in a circle—rotate your wood counterclockwise. Remove the blade and test the fit of the circular bottom piece into the hole in the top piece of wood. Adjust the angle of your saw table until the pieces fit flush with each other.

Cutting the inlay

When inlaying multiple colors of wood, it's important to take each step slowly and make sure each stage is glued and dried completely before moving to the next step. Sand the bottom of the design between each step to ensure the wood is flat. Attach your pattern to the white wood. Stack the first two pieces of stock as you did with the test pieces and cut the inlay details. If sections overlap, such as the button and scarf, start with the element of the design that is farthest back first. For example, on the short snowman, inlay his scarf first, then add the button. As you cut each color of the inlay, push the pieces up through the holes in the white wood. Use wood glue to join the inlay pieces and allow the glue to dry before moving on to the next inlay. Use a copy of the pattern to trace any missing pattern lines onto the glued stock.

Once the inlay is complete, drill the holes for the buttons, eyes, and hanger. Return the table to square and cut around the perimeter of the ornaments. Hide any blade-entry holes by filling them with white glue and sawdust. Then sand the ornaments flat. Use a woodburner or permanent marker to add the thread lines on the buttons. Apply tung oil to the completed ornament and add the hanging string.

Inlay snowmen patterns

Photocopy at 100%

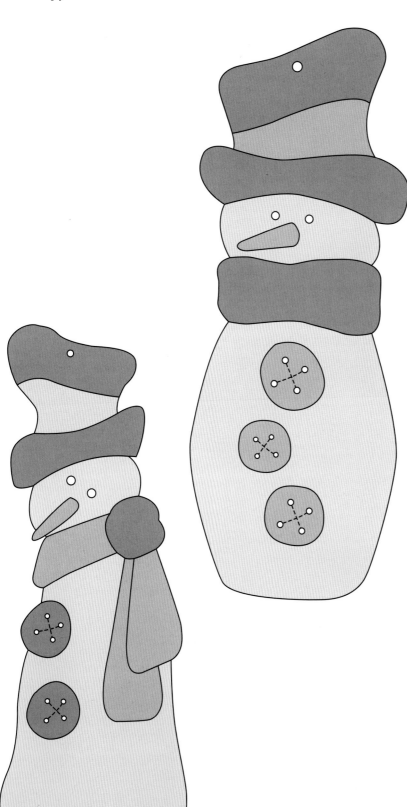

Amazing 3-D Christmas Ornaments

By Sue Mey

Compound-cut ornaments make fun and easy holiday presents. The ornaments can be made from a solid piece of wood and painted or stained or finished naturally. To give the ornaments a unique look, glue up your blank using thin strips of contrasting wood.

I cut my stock slightly oversized and sand it down to 1¾" by 1¾"(45mm by 45mm). For straight blade-entry holes and neat inside cuts, the blocks must have perfectly straight edges at a 90° angle to each other. If you are not laminating your blank for a multicolored ornament, you can skip right to step three.

1 **Cut the strips to size.** I cut an assortment of ¼" to ⅜"-thick wood into 1⅞"-wide strips. Cut the strips into 5½"-long pieces. Shorter pieces can be used for smaller ornaments.

2 **Glue the strips together.** Mix and match the strips of wood for unique color combinations. The stack should be about 2" thick. Apply wood glue between the layers and clamp the strips together until the glue dries.

3 **Prepare the blank.** Sand or trim the blank down to 1¾" by 1¾". I use a disc sander, but you can use a table saw or your method of choice. It is critical that the sides be flat and square to each other.

4 **Drill the blade-entry holes.** Cover the blank with masking tape. Fold the pattern on the dotted line and attach the pattern to the blank. Drill the blade-entry holes with a ⅛"-diameter bit. Remove the rough edges with sandpaper or a scraper.

5 **Cut the fretwork.** I use a #9 blade for soft woods and a #12 blade for the laminated blanks. Cut the frets on one side, remove the waste, and then turn the blank and cut the frets on the adjoining side.

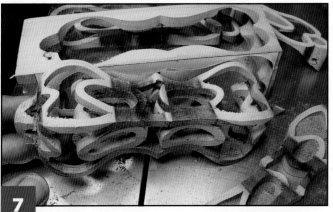

6 **Cut the perimeter.** Start with the end-grain area. Cut the entire perimeter on one side. Then hold the ornament and waste in place while you wrap clear tape around the blank. Rotate the blank and cut the perimeter of the ornament on the second side.

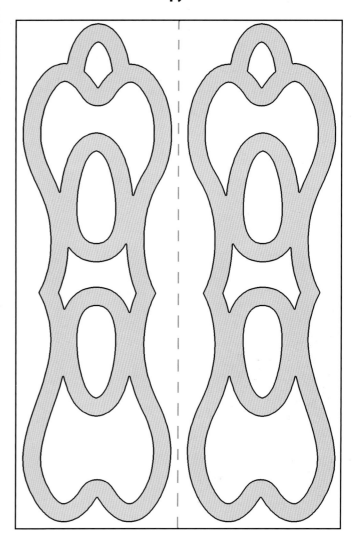

Photocopy at 100%

7 **Finish the ornament.** Remove the waste wood and sand the ornament with 320-grit sandpaper or needle files. Remove the sanding dust with a stiff-bristled paintbrush and apply a deep-penetrating furniture wax or Danish oil. Allow the finish to dry and remove any excess with a dry lint-free cloth. Then apply several thin coats of clear varnish.

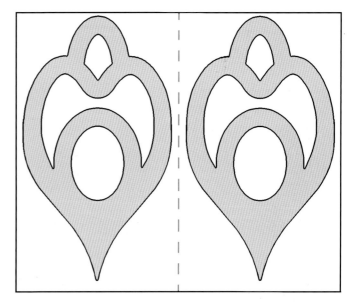

materials & tools

MATERIALS:

- 1¾" x 1¾" x 5⁵⁄₁₆" wood of choice (large ornaments)
- 1¾" x 1¾" x 4⅛" wood of choice (medium ornaments)
- 1¾" x 1¾" x 3" wood of choice (small ornaments)
- Masking tape
- Temporary-bond spray adhesive or glue stick
- Wood glue (laminating strips of hardwood)
- Clear packing tape
- Sandpaper, assorted grits

- Deep-penetrating furniture wax liquid or Danish oil
- Lint-free cloth
- Clear spray varnish
- 320-grit sandpaper

TOOLS:

- #9 and #12 skip-tooth blades or blades of choice
- Drill press with ⅛"-diameter bit
- Disc sander
- Needle files
- Stiff-bristled paintbrush
- Medium-sized artist's brush

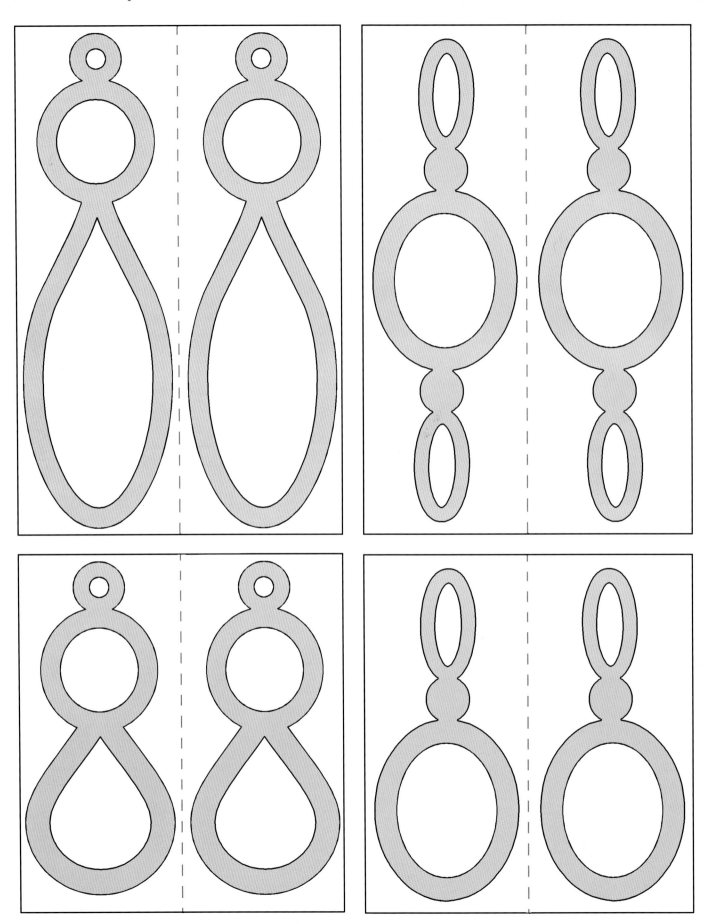

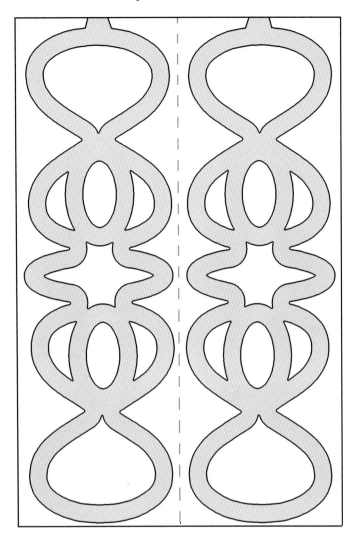

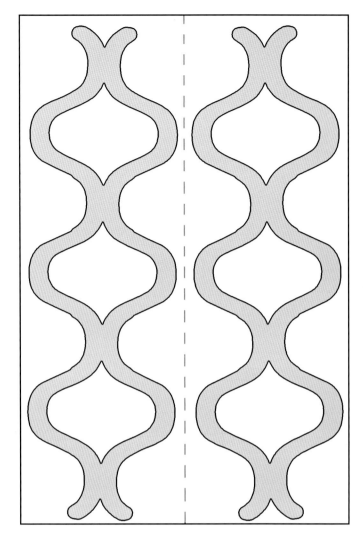

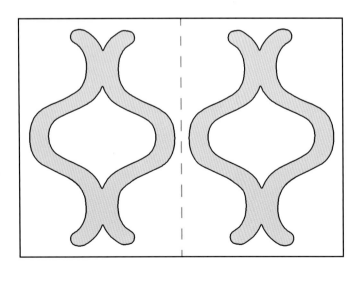

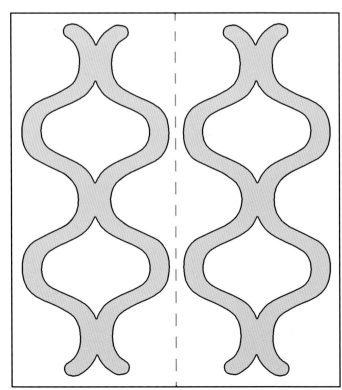

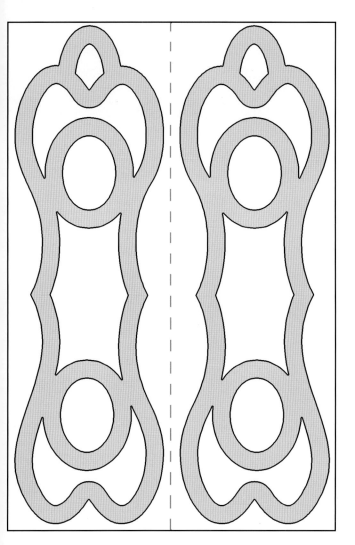

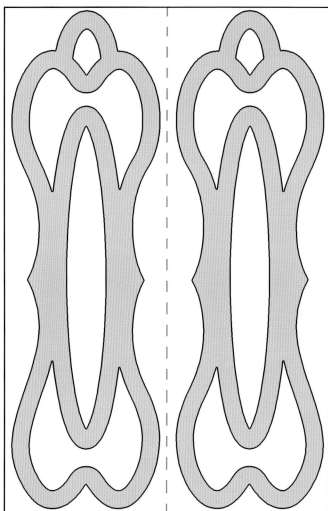

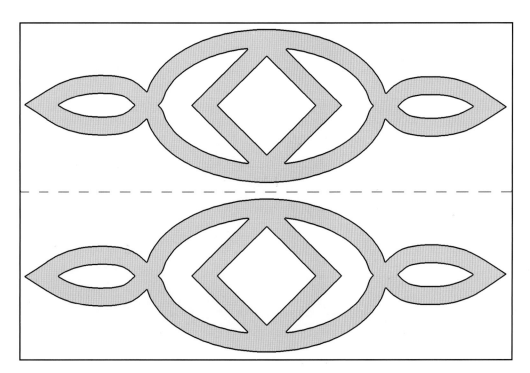

12-Piece Intarsia Nativity Set

By Kathy Wise

Create these beautiful Nativity ornaments from leftover pieces of expensive hardwoods. You can create a full set for everyone on your list. Another option is to give the ornaments individually or in groups over several years. Your family and friends will eagerly await the next installment in the series.

Use double-sided tape to attach two pieces of wood and stack cut two ornaments at once to reduce your production time. The small size eliminates the need for a backing board. I added the facial details with a woodburner. You could also cut these details. Enlarge the patterns for a totally different look.

Step 1: Prepare the patterns and wood. Make several photocopies of the patterns. Apply spray adhesive to the back of the paper patterns, and position them on the shiny side of the contact paper. Peel the backing off the contact paper and position it on the wood.

Step 2: Cut the pieces. Use a #5 reverse-tooth blade or your blade of choice. Check a cut piece with a small square to ensure that the saw table is square to the blade. Switch to a #3 reverse-tooth blade for the intricate areas. Mark the back of each piece, and place it on the master pattern.

▲ Step 3: Check the fit and color of the pieces. Mix and match the colors of the pieces and make sure you like the fit and color of each piece. Now is the time to make adjustments or cut new pieces.

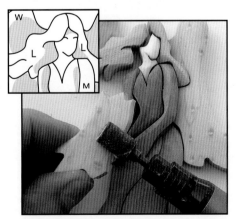

▲ Step 4: Sand and shape each piece. Use the sanding guide as a reference; the grey shaded areas on the pattern are lower than the white areas. Use a pneumatic drum sander

or a ½"-diameter sanding drum in a rotary power carver or air grinder. The angel's wings, for example, are shaped so they are thinner as they get close to the angel's body to add to the illusion that they are attached to her back. Use needle-nose pliers or tweezers to hold the small pieces. Buff the pieces with a 220-grit sanding mop after sanding and shaping them.

Step 5: Glue the pieces together. Apply cyanoacrylate (CA) glue to the sides of the pieces and place them in position. You may add wood filler to the back to fill in gaps and provide additional strength.

▲ Step 6: Finish the piece. Woodburn any details, such as facial features, that were not cut out.

Step 7: Apply several coats of spray varnish. Add embellishments, such as paint, rhinestones or gold leaf, if you choose, before applying the varnish. To add glitter, spray on a coat of varnish and sprinkle the glitter on while the varnish is wet. After the varnish dries, apply another coat.

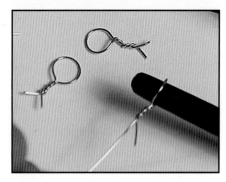

▲ Step 8: Add the hangers. Drill a ¹⁄₁₆"-diameter hole in the top of the ornament. Glue or screw an eyelet into the hole. I make eyelets from fine gauge wire wrapped around a paintbrush handle. Glue the eyelet in place with CA glue.

materials & tools

MATERIALS:
- Assorted scraps ranging from ⅛" to ½"-thick and measuring up to 5" x 5"
- Spray varnish or finish of choice
- Clear contact paper
- Spray adhesive
- Fine wire or screw eyelets
- Cyanoacrylate glue
- Wood filler (optional)
- Embellishments of choice (glitter, rhinestones, paint, gold leaf, etc.)

TOOLS:
- #3 & #5 reverse-tooth blades or blades of choice
- Drill with ¹⁄₁₆"-diameter bit
- Pneumatic drum sander and/or rotary power carver or air grinder with ½"-diameter sanding drum
- Tweezers or needle nose pliers

Mary

Light areas of robe:
Brazilian tulipwood
Dark areas of robe:
Bloodwood
Hands & face: Poplar

Angel

Gown: Pink ivory
Wings: Bird's eye
  maple
Hair: Yellowheart
Hands & face: Poplar

Infant Jesus

Straw: Yellowheart
Infant: Poplar
Blanket: Bloodwood
Manger: Black walnut

Shepherd

Light areas of robe:
  Ash
Headdress & dark
  areas of robe: Beech
Hands & face: Poplar
Staff: Black walnut;
  you may need to carve
  away a little wood on
  the staff where the
  hand grips it.

Joseph

Light areas of robe:
  Sycamore
Headdress & dark
  areas of robe: Beech
Staff & beard:
  Black walnut
Hands, feet, & face:
  Poplar

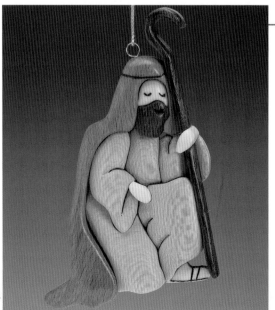

Lamb

Body & top of head:
  Poplar
Face: Black walnut

Camel

Camel: Beech
Eye: Ebony

Wise man 1

Robe: Zebrawood
Cape: Black walnut
Crown: Yellowheart
Beard & gift: Wenge
Hands & Face: Poplar

Wise man 2

Robe: Canarywood
Cape: Cocobolo
Lower part of crown:
 Yellowheart
Top of crown: Cocobolo
Beard & gift: Wenge
Hands & Face: Poplar

Cow

Body, tail, & head:
 Cherry
Horns: Poplar
Eye: Ebony

Donkey

Body: Black walnut
Forelock & mane:
 Wenge
Eye: Ebony

Wise man 3

Dark part of robe:
 Lacewood
Headdress & light areas
 of robe: Cedar
Crown: Yellowheart
Beard & Gift: Wenge
Hands & Face: Poplar

Nativity patterns

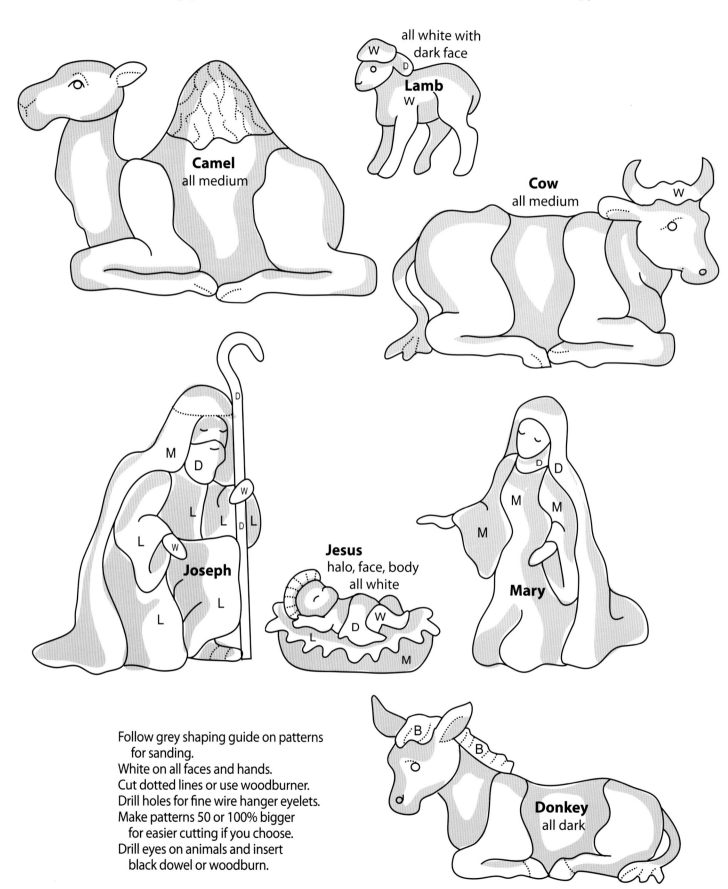

Camel
all medium

all white with
dark face

Lamb
W

W   D

Cow
all medium

W

Joseph

D

M   D

L   L   L

L   W   D

L

L

Jesus
halo, face, body
all white

L   D   W

M

Mary

D   D

M   M

M

Donkey
all dark

B

B

Follow grey shaping guide on patterns
   for sanding.
White on all faces and hands.
Cut dotted lines or use woodburner.
Drill holes for fine wire hanger eyelets.
Make patterns 50 or 100% bigger
   for easier cutting if you choose.
Drill eyes on animals and insert
   black dowel or woodburn.

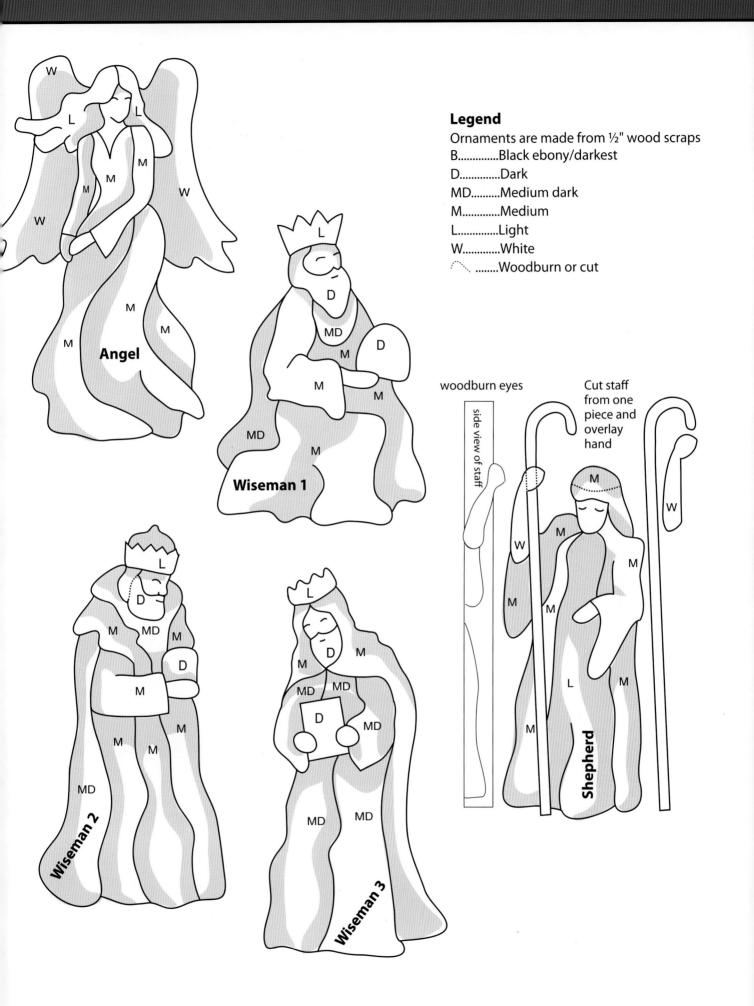

Legend

Ornaments are made from ½" wood scraps

B.............Black ebony/darkest
D.............Dark
MD.........Medium dark
M............Medium
L.............Light
W............White
⌣ ....Woodburn or cut

Angel

Wiseman 1

Wiseman 2

Wiseman 3

woodburn eyes

side view of staff

Cut staff from one piece and overlay hand

Shepherd

Whimsical Christmas Ornaments

By Kathy Wise

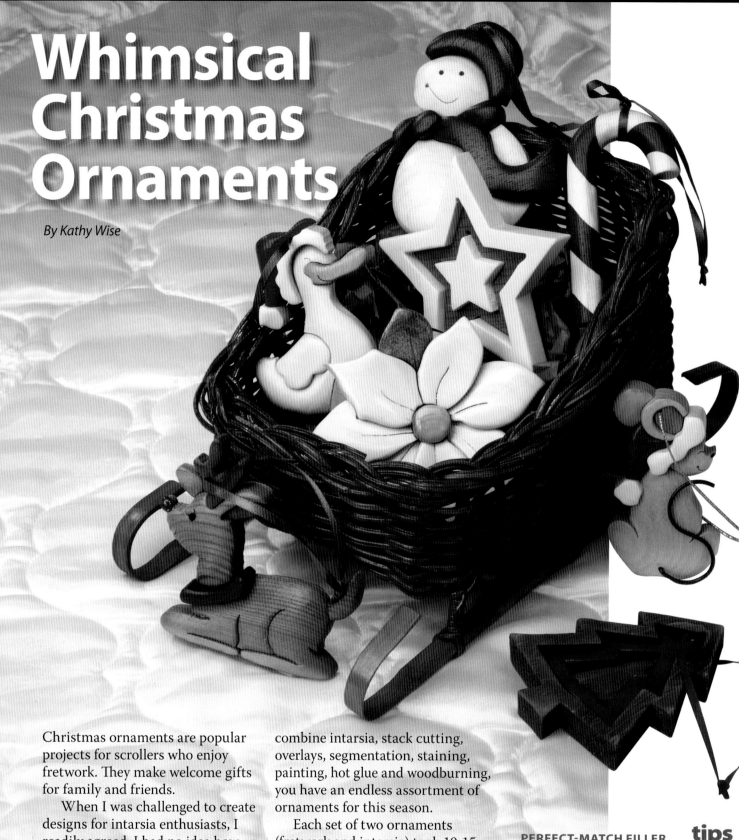

Christmas ornaments are popular projects for scrollers who enjoy fretwork. They make welcome gifts for family and friends.

When I was challenged to create designs for intarsia enthusiasts, I readily agreed. I had no idea how much fun this assignment would be. Not only did it use up some of my scrap wood, but it really allowed me to get creative and experiment with different scrolling styles. If you combine intarsia, stack cutting, overlays, segmentation, staining, painting, hot glue and woodburning, you have an endless assortment of ornaments for this season.

Each set of two ornaments (fretwork and intarsia) took 10-15 minutes to cut. I've included basic instructions to cut intarsia and fretwork and shown some variations on each pattern to stimulate your imagination.

tips

PERFECT-MATCH FILLER

When cutting intarsia projects, if you have any gaps or open areas, mix instant glue with sawdust for a perfectly-matched wood filler that dries quickly.

Snowman

Intarsia. Cut the hat and scarf separately from contrasting wood or try staining or painting these pieces.

Fretwork. You can add extra details by cutting out little pieces of black wood or plastic as overlays for the buttons and nose. Fill in the hat and scarf with different colors of glitter glue. To fill the hat and scarf, put a piece of transparent tape on the backside of the cutouts. Fill the openings with hot glitter glue, using a toothpick to push it into the corners. After the glue is dry, remove the tape.

Mouse

Intarsia. Sand and round the edges. Use a ½" or ¼"-diameter sanding drum to sand around the nose and tail. Paint or stain the hat. For the tail, paint aluminum wire brown, and bend it into the curved tail shape. I use a woodburner to give the mouse a little black nose.

Fretwork. After cutting the pieces, apply your finish of choice. For a different look, fill the inside of the hat with glitter glue, or add a dab of white cotton fluff to the hat.

Bird and Wreath

Intarsia. For added texture, sand both the outside and the inside edges of the wreath. Use red dowels for the berries or stain the dowels red. Darken the eyes and beak with a woodburner. I use lignavitae vera wood for the wreath. It's an exotic hardwood that turns green when exposed to sunlight.

Fretwork. Again, I use a woodburner to add texture and dimension to the bird. Stain the wreath slightly darker than the bird.

Duck

Intarsia. I stack cut a piece of yellowheart with a piece of poplar and swapped out the pieces. The feet and beak were cut from a piece of scrap mahogany, and the cap was cut from a scrap of lignavitae vera. Or you can stain or paint your Santa hat red for a bright eye-catching ornament. You can make the eyes closed, as shown in the pattern, or open by adding a small hole.

Fretwork. These little ducks look great with a coat of paint. Fill in the cap with glitter glue, paint the duck white, and the bill and feet orange. The technique for filling an area with glitter glue is explained in the instructions for the snowman ornament.

Cat

Intarsia. Sand and shape the pieces using the shaping guide as a reference. For a simple bow, cut it out as one piece. For a more complex bow, cut the red lines to divide it into sections. Taper the tail to fit the body.

Fretwork. Add details to the fretwork with a woodburner. Or cut an overlay bow from veneer or a different color of wood. You can also fill the bow with hot glitter glue.

Dog

Intarsia. Use a different color of wood or paint the hat before gluing the pieces together with instant glue. Round the edges of the tail, and taper the end down to the same level as the body. Use the shaping guide as a reference.

Fretwork. Use glitter glue to fill in the dog's hat and embellish the fur trim with glitter or cotton. You can also use acrylic paints to add details and customize the ornament.

Poinsettia

Intarsia. Use different colors of hardwood or use a white wood, such as basswood or poplar, and stain the different parts. Shape the pieces, using the pattern as a guide. Use a small sanding drum to add the texture to the inside of the petals.

Fretwork. Color the pieces, using your paint or stain of choice. I add a veneer backing. Glue the ornament to the sheet of veneer with instant glue. Cut around the perimeter of the ornament with a sharp hobby knife or wait to cut the perimeter until you have attached the backing.

Pig

Intarsia. Use a different color of wood or paint the hat before gluing the pieces together with instant glue. Round the edges of the tail, and taper the end down to the same level as the body. Use the shaping guide as a reference. I use pink ivory for the body of the pig.

Fretwork. Fill in the hat with different colors of glitter glue.

Deer

Intarsia. Mix and match the colors to change the antlers and the inside of the ear. For a black eye, burn the end of a toothpick, and insert it into the eye. Use glitter glue to color the collar red and to make the nose sparkle.

Fretwork. Finish the fretwork deer with a natural finish. Then apply a little red glitter glue to the tip of the nose and collar. I also hot-glue bells onto the collar.

Candy Cane

Intarsia. The intarsia version of the candy cane is demonstrated in the step-by-step instructions. Stack cut red and white wood and interchange the pieces. Glue together before sanding. Round the edges on the top or top and bottom for a round candy cane.

Fretwork. Fill the negative spaces with glitter glue or leave them open for a natural look. Cut a solid candy cane from red wood or add a backing board painted red behind the fretwork cane.

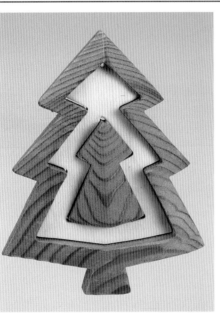

Tree and Star

Intarsia. Stack cut different colors, and interchange the pieces. Sand the outer and inner star and tree sections. Taper the outside edges of the tree. You can also stain or paint the different sections.

Fretwork. Stack cut several trees or stars at once. Drill a blade-entry hole at the top and use it for the ribbon. Using a #2 or #3 blade, cut out the inside star and interchange pieces or use as separate ornaments. Spray paint, stain or use clear varnish to finish the ornaments.

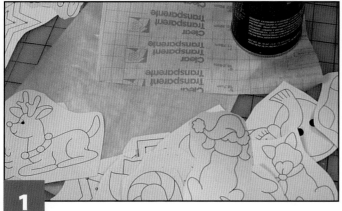

1 Organize your patterns and blanks. Make several copies of each pattern. Apply spray adhesive to the back of the pattern, and attach it to the contact paper. Peel off the backing paper from the contact paper, and apply it to the clean, dry wood.

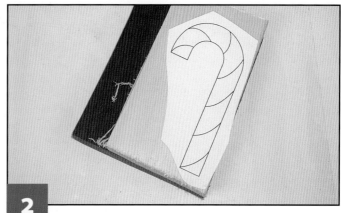

2 Assemble blanks for stack cutting. For an intarsia ornament, stack two ½"-thick pieces of contrasting wood together, using double-sided tape. Be sure the wood is flat when stacking, or it will distort the cuts. Stack three to six thin pieces together for fretwork ornaments.

3 Cut out the pieces. Make sure your blade is square to the table. Use a #5 reverse-tooth blade for most of the cutting, but switch to a #3 reverse-tooth blade for the more detailed cuts. Mark the back of the piece, and place it on the master pattern.

4 Mix and match the colors, and glue the pieces together. (Note: The candy cane ornament is glued first, then shaped. Most of the other ornaments will be glued after shaping the individual pieces.) Use instant glue for the ornaments that will have a natural finish. For painted ornaments, use your wood glue of choice prior to painting.

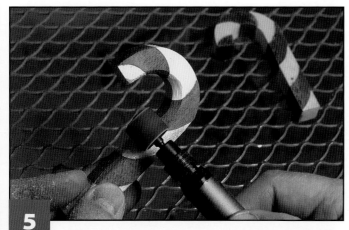

5 Sand and shape the ornaments. Add texture to the intarsia ornaments. I use a ½"-diameter sanding drum or a pneumatic sanding drum. Follow up with a sanding mop for a polished finish. Drill holes for the strings on all the ornaments.

6 Apply your finish of choice. I apply a spray varnish or lacquer. You can paint the ornaments or apply a stain as well. Attach bells, string, and any other embellishments with hot glue. Feel free to experiment with different types of paints and finishes to achieve the result you want.

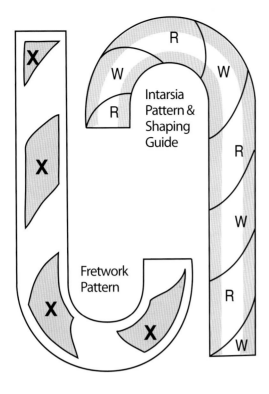

Intarsia
Pattern &
Shaping
Guide

Fretwork
Pattern

**Whimsical ornament
patterns**

Photocopy at 100%

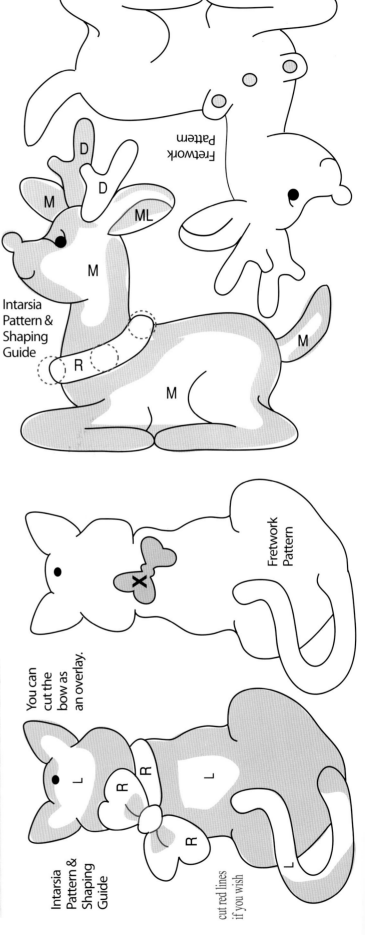

Fretwork Pattern

Intarsia
Pattern &
Shaping
Guide

Intarsia Pattern &
Shaping Guide

Fretwork Pattern

You can cut the bow as an overlay.

cut red lines if you wish

materials
& tools

MATERIALS:
- Assorted scraps ⅛" to ½" thick
  and up to 5" x 5" in assorted
  colors
- Finish of choice: Spray varnish or
  lacquer, paint, or stain
- Roll of clear shelf contact paper
- Spray adhesive
- Yellow wood glue
- Instant glue
- Glitter glue sticks, red & green
  (for hot glue gun)
- Transparent tape

TOOLS:
- #3 & #5 reverse-tooth blades or
  blades of choice
- Drill with assorted small drill bits
- Pneumatic drum sander, ½"
  and ¼"-diameter sanding drums
- Hot melt glue gun

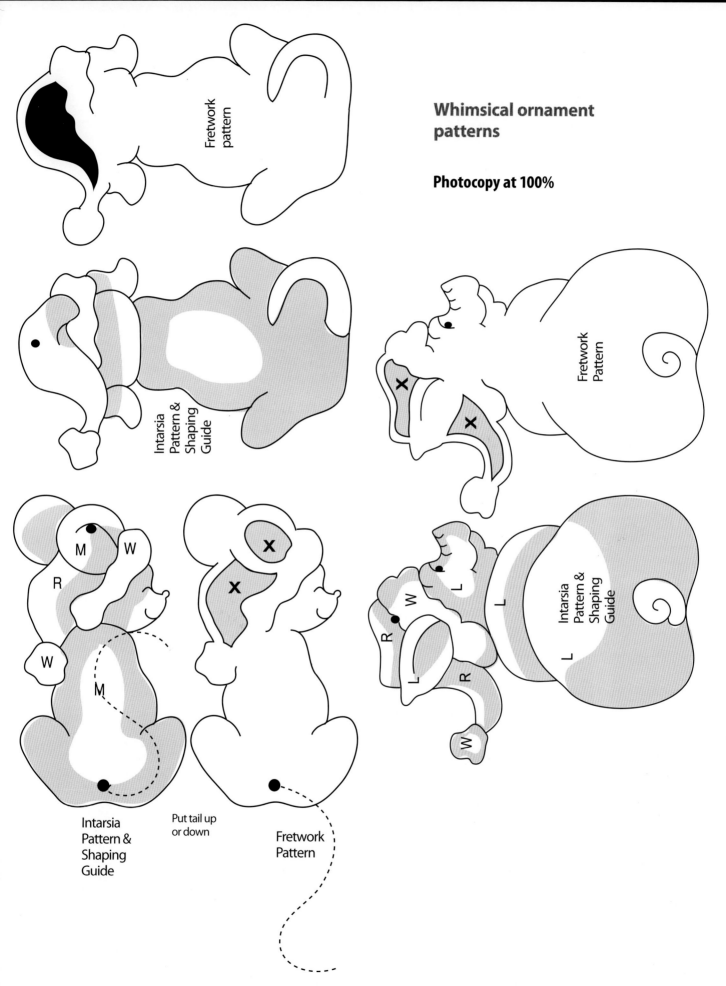

Whimsical ornament patterns

Photocopy at 100%

Fretwork pattern

Fretwork Pattern

Intarsia Pattern & Shaping Guide

Intarsia Pattern & Shaping Guide

R
M
W
W
M

Intarsia Pattern & Shaping Guide

X
X

Put tail up or down

Fretwork Pattern

L
W
L
R
L
R
W

Intarsia Pattern & Shaping Guide

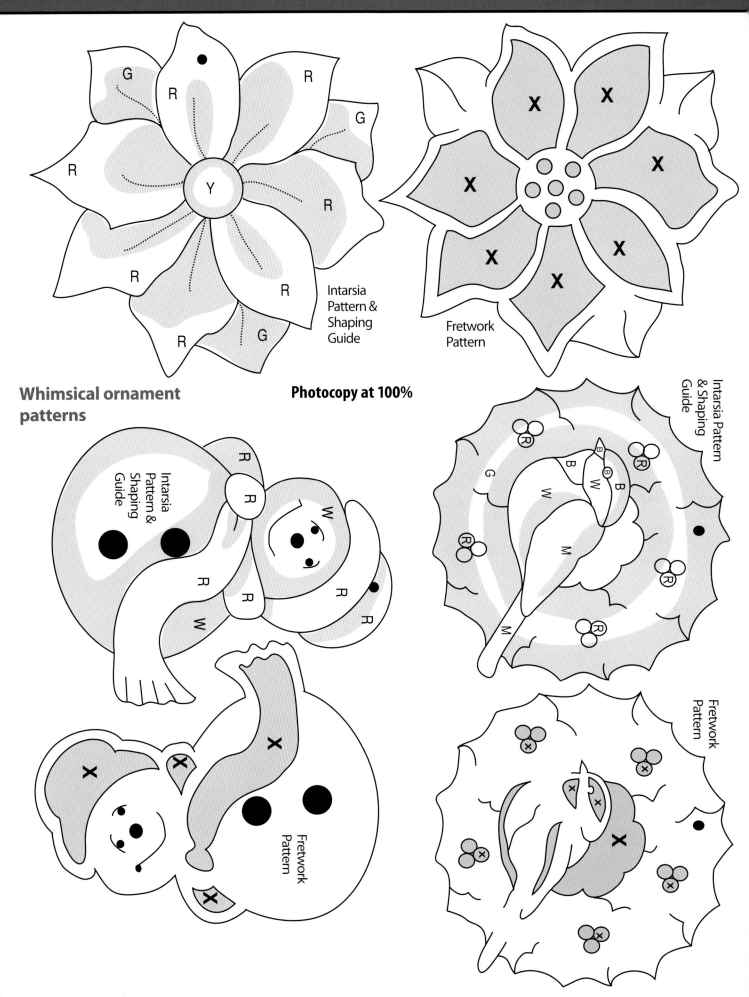

Whimsical ornament patterns

Photocopy at 100%

Intarsia Pattern & Shaping Guide

Fretwork Pattern

Intarsia Pattern & Shaping Guide

Intarsia Pattern & Shaping Guide

Fretwork Pattern

Fretwork Pattern

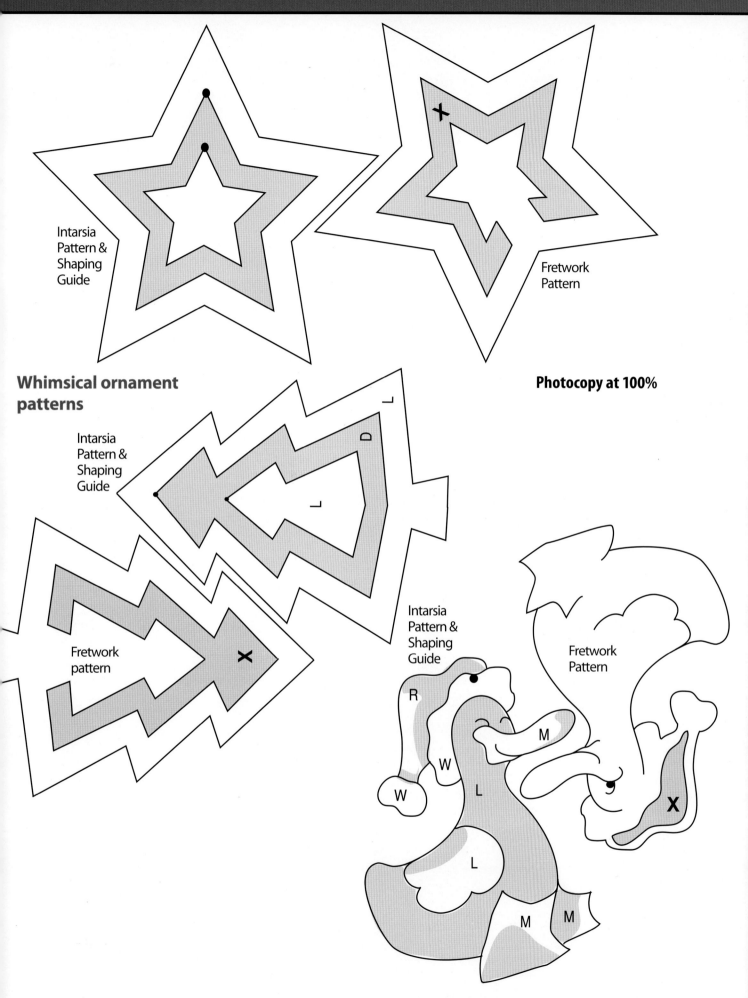

Intarsia
Pattern &
Shaping
Guide

Fretwork
Pattern

**Whimsical ornament
patterns**

Photocopy at 100%

Intarsia
Pattern &
Shaping
Guide

Fretwork
pattern

Intarsia
Pattern &
Shaping
Guide

Fretwork
Pattern

Santa's Workshop Ornaments

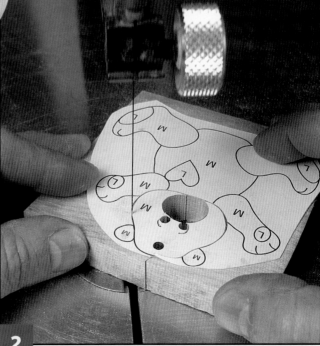

1 **Transfer the pattern to the blank.** Apply spray adhesive to the back of the pattern and stick it to the shiny side of the contact paper. Peel off the paper backing and position the pattern on the wood. To stack cut, use double-sided tape to attach two ½"-thick pieces of wood together.

By Kathy Wise

Christmas ornaments are always a big hit for holiday gift giving. With these fun designs from Santa's workshop, you can use scrap wood to make a set for everyone on your list. Choose from toy shop elves, a rocking horse, a drum, a jack-in-the-box, or a teddy bear. Use wood with a variety of exotic colors or figures to make each ornament unique.

Each pair of ornaments takes about ten minutes to cut. The basic steps are the same for all of the ornaments. To increase your production, stack cut two pieces of contrasting wood and mix and match the pieces for a pair of perfect-fitting ornaments. It is important to have flat wood for a good cut and fit. Sand any uneven areas flat on your scrap pieces. Always keep a copy of the pattern for future use.

2 **Cut the pieces.** Be sure your blade of choice is square to the saw table. I use a #3 reverse-tooth blade. Mark the back of each piece and place it on a copy of the pattern. Check the fit of the pieces as you go and make any necessary adjustments. If you don't like the color or fit of a piece, cut a replacement.

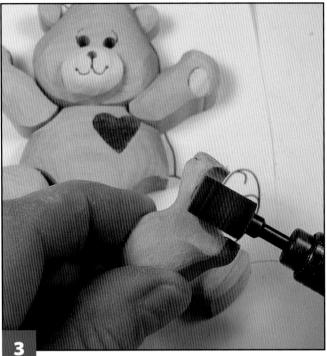

3

Shape the pieces. Refer to the shaping guide on the pattern. The grey shaded areas are lower than the white areas. Use forceps or tweezers to hold small pieces while you shape them on a pneumatic drum sander or shape the small pieces with a rotary power carver. Buff each piece on a sanding mop for a polished finish. Sand the back of the pieces flat.

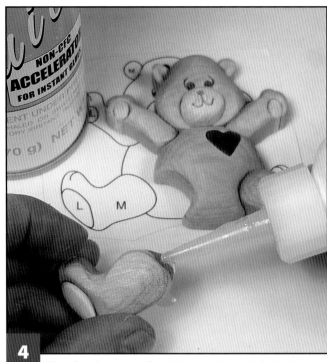

4

Glue the pieces together. Paint or stain any individual pieces. Use cyanoacrylate (CA) glue to attach the pieces together. A backer board is not necessary. Use wood filler on the back to seal any small gaps and help strengthen the ornament. Make sure the wood filler does not squeeze through between the pieces and become visible from the front of the ornament.

5

Finish the ornament. Drill small holes for the eyelets. You can add details, such as stitching on the bear, with a woodburner. Spray the ornaments with your finish of choice. Twist fine wire around a paintbrush handle to make your own eyelets. Glue the eyelets into the holes. Attach the string and sign the back.

materials & tools

MATERIALS:

- ⅛" to ½" x 5" x 5" assorted colors of scrap wood, try to get a good assortment of colors and figures
- Finish of choice (spray varnish or lacquer, paint, or stain)
- Roll of clear contact paper
- Spray adhesive
- Fine wire for eyelets
- Cyanoacrylate glue

TOOLS:

- #3 reverse-tooth blades or blades of choice
- Drill with ⅟₁₆"-diameter bit (eyelet holes)
- Pneumatic drum sander or rotary power carver with a ½"-diameter sanding drum
- Mop sander
- Woodburner (optional)

Santa's workshop ornament patterns

Photocopy at 100%

Legend

Start with ½" thick wood

B............Black/darkest

D............Dark

R............ Reddish

M............Medium

      (Green on elves)

Y............Yellow

L............Light

W............White

     Shaping guide

     Woodburned details

Drill holes for eyes and insert black dowels. You can woodburn or stain if you don't have ebony.

Make buttons black

L use dowels

Decorations

Christmas is all about the personal touch, which is why any of the projects in this section, made with love on your scroll saw, would be an excellent addition to a home's holiday décor. There are candleholders, nativity scenes, signs, wreaths, Santas—even three different kinds of make-your-own "Christmas trees." Make them for yourself or as gifts—there's a wealth of fretwork and intarsia subjects to choose from, with a mix of easy and more challenging projects. Whether you choose a traditional theme or one that reflects a more whimsical approach to the holiday, it's sure to communicate that you care.

Poinsettia Wreath,
by Kathy Wise, page 142.

Festive
Silhouettes
Illuminate
Your Home

By Paul Meisel

Brighten up the holidays with these colorful votive holders. Dancing candlelight shines through the transparent colored acrylic to illuminate the fretwork design.

Patterns are provided for both Christian and Jewish symbols. The silhouettes are cut from ¼"-thick wood, so it's easy to stack cut them to speed up production.

Each project consists of three parts: a base that holds the candle cup, a front piece with the fretwork silhouette, and the colored acrylic backer used to diffuse the light.

Step 1: Cut the front pieces.
Attach a photocopy of the pattern to the stock. Drill blade-entry holes with a ¹⁄₁₆"-diameter drill bit. Cut the fretwork. Then cut around the perimeter using your #5 reverse-tooth blade of choice.

Step 2: Paint the front pieces.
Paint or stain the front pieces as desired. I apply white latex primer followed by a coat of white acrylic latex paint.

Step 3: Cut the acrylic backer.
Attach the pattern to the acrylic. You will only be cutting along the red line. Set your saw to a medium speed and use a #5 reverse-tooth blade. Clear packaging tape over the pattern will help lubricate the blade and deter the acrylic from melting as it is being cut.

Step 4: Cut and shape the base.
I make several bases at once. Start with a piece of ¾" by 4½" by 36" pine. Cut a ⅜" by ⅜" dado ⅝" from one edge. Use a table saw or a

router with a ⅜"-diameter bit. Cut the bases to the proper length. Tilt the table-saw blade to 45° or use a 45° chamfer bit in a router to chamfer the edges of the base.

Step 5: Finish the base. Use a ⅞"-diameter Forstner bit to drill the ⅝"-deep hole for the votive candle cup. Sand the base and apply a coat of sanding sealer. Lightly sand it again and apply a coat of polyurethane.

Step 6: Assembling the project.
Position a piece of acrylic behind
the fretwork front and slide the two
pieces into the dado in the base.
Do not glue the pieces into the
groove. The project is designed to
be disassembled for storage after
the holidays. Cut an assortment of
colors for the acrylic backing and
try placing different colors behind
each silhouette. The silhouettes and
colored acrylic are interchangeable.
Insert the glass votive in the hole on
the base and add a votive candle of
your choice.

POLISHING ACRYLIC   **tips**

*Polish the edges of your acrylic with a
propane torch. Sand the edges with 220-
grit or finer sandpaper and remove any
protective paper or plastic. Clamp a piece
of scrap in a vise to practice the technique.
Light the torch and pass the flame over the
edge of the acrylic. Don't get too close or
hold the flame in one place too long—this
will damage the acrylic. After a little
experimentation, you will determine how
far to hold the torch from the acrylic and
how fast to move the flame. The edge of
the acrylic will melt just enough to give a
polished appearance.*

Silhouette panel patterns

Red line - acrylic backer

Black line - front panel

Photocopy at 100%

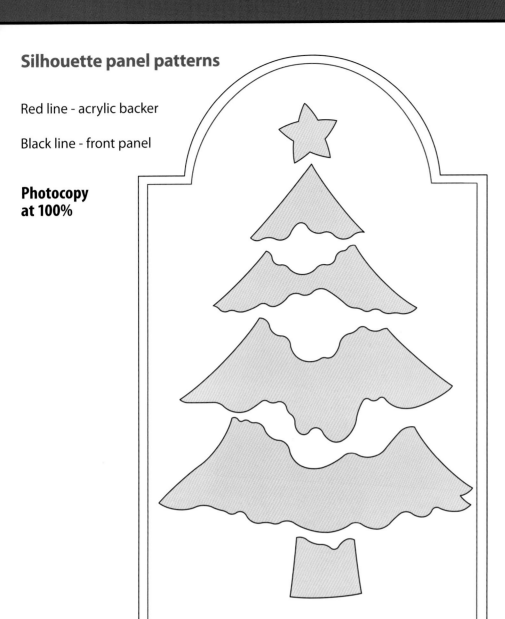

materials & tools

MATERIALS:
- Glass votive candle cup*
- Colored acrylic plastic set*
- ¾" x 4½" x 4½" pine (per base)
- ¼" x 3¾" x 6⅛" plywood or wood of choice (per silhouette)
- Assorted sandpaper up to 220 grit
- White latex primer and paint
- Sanding sealer
- Polyurethane

TOOLS:
- Table saw (optional)
- Miter saw (optional)
- Router with ⅜"-diameter straight bit and chamfer bit (optional)
- #5 reverse-tooth blades of choice
- Drill press with 1/16"-diameter bit
- Propane torch
- ⅞"-diameter Forstner bit*
- Paintbrushes

SPECIAL SOURCES:
Items marked with an asterisk are available from *www.meiselwoodhobby.com*, or 800-441-9870.

Festive silhouettes ornament patterns

Photocopy at 100%

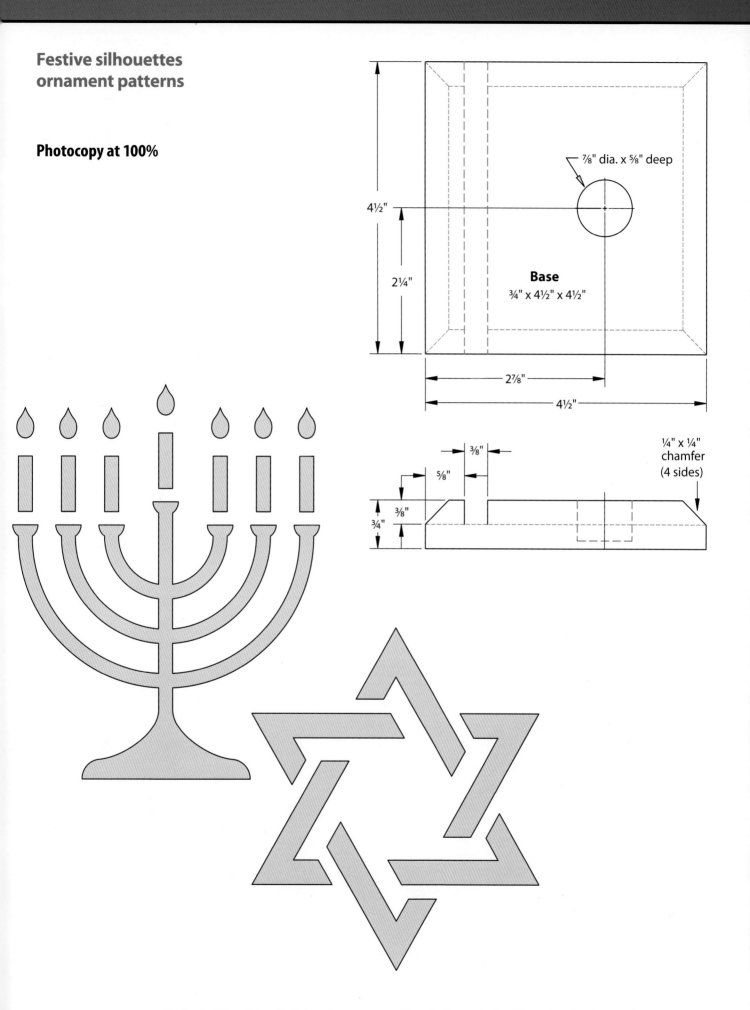

7/8" dia. x 5/8" deep

4½"

2¼"

Base
¾" x 4½" x 4½"

2⅞"

4½"

3/8"

5/8"

3/8"

¾"

¼" x ¼" chamfer (4 sides)

Winter Woodland Lighted Arch

By Tom Sevy
Pattern by Volker Arnold

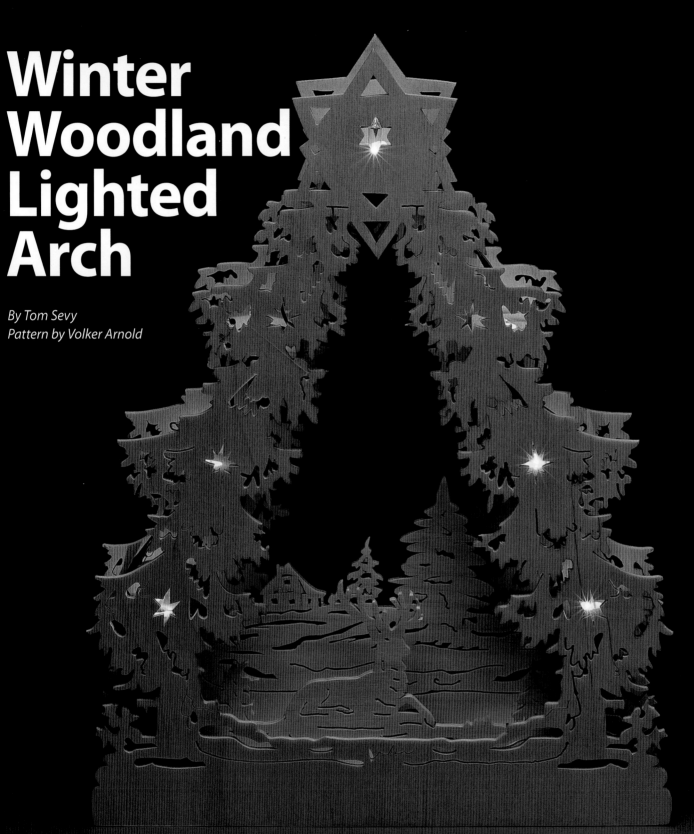

Get a head start on the Christmas season with this charming layered display. Twinkling lights and rolling, snow-covered hills set the tone for this lighted arch, which is modeled after traditional German lichterböegen.

The size of the project can easily be adjusted to suit your taste. If you enlarge the pattern, use ¼"- instead of ⅛"-thick wood. Remember to enlarge the spacers in proportion with the rest of the project. The slots for the interior scenes must be adjusted as well. The diameter of the holes for the electric lights remains the same.

Step 1: Cut the fretwork. Use masking tape to attach the stock for two arches together. Attach the pattern to the stack with spray adhesive. Drill blade-entry holes and cut the fretwork. Cut the large center area last. The bottom of the arches must be perfectly flat; cut outside the line and sand up to it if necessary.

Step 2: Cut the spacers. Determine the size of the light sockets. Drill holes the same diameter as the light sockets in the spacers. Then cut the spacers. You can stack cut several spacers at once. Only the bottom three spacers need the slots for the inserts. Make sure all of the spacers are the same size.

Step 3: Glue the spacers to the back arch. Use cyanoacrylate (CA) glue. Align the spacers on the bottom flush with the bottom of the arch. Make sure the slots face the top of the arch to accommodate the deer and village inserts. Use the dotted lines on the pattern as a guide for spacer placement.

Step 4: Assemble the project. Install the inserts before attaching the second arch. The village insert fits in the back slot and the deer insert fits into the front slot. A drop of CA glue will lock the inserts in place. Add a bit of CA glue to the end of all of the spacers, place the front arch in position, and hold it in place until the glue dries.

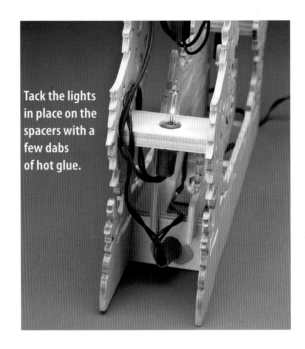

Tack the lights in place on the spacers with a few dabs of hot glue.

Step 5: Apply a finish. Traditionally, lichterböegen were left unfinished. You can stain the inserts for additional contrast or apply an oil finish to the entire project. I seal everything with spray lacquer, which hides any CA glue that squeezed out of the joints.

Step 6: Install the lights. Thread the lights, beginning at the bottom, following around the arch, and ending back where you started. After the lights are in position, lock them in place with hot glue. Secure any hanging wires to the spacers with a dab of hot glue to keep them tucked up out of sight. Do not get glue on the lights, and make sure the lights do not touch any wood.

Winter woodland arch patterns

Deer insert
Cut 1

Village insert
Cut 1

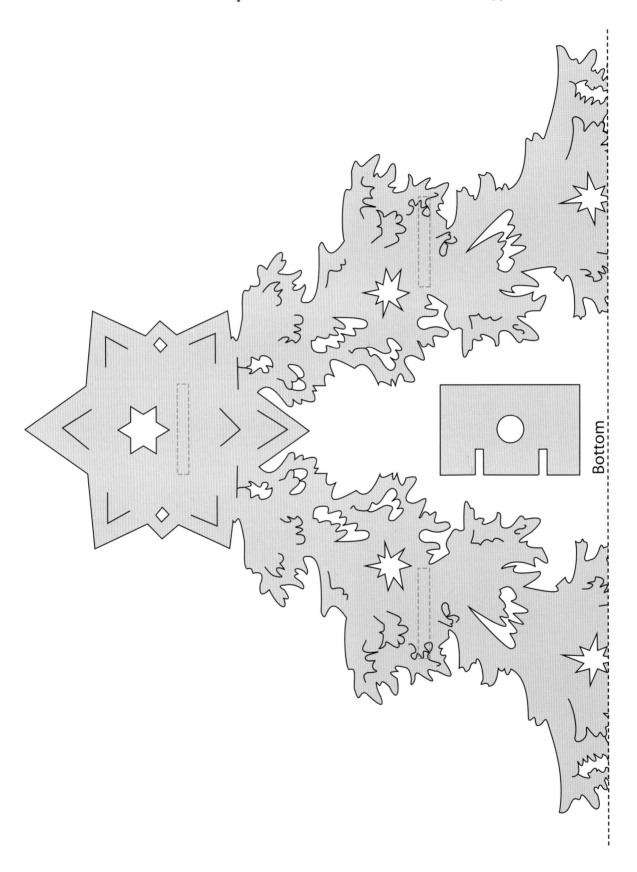

Bottom

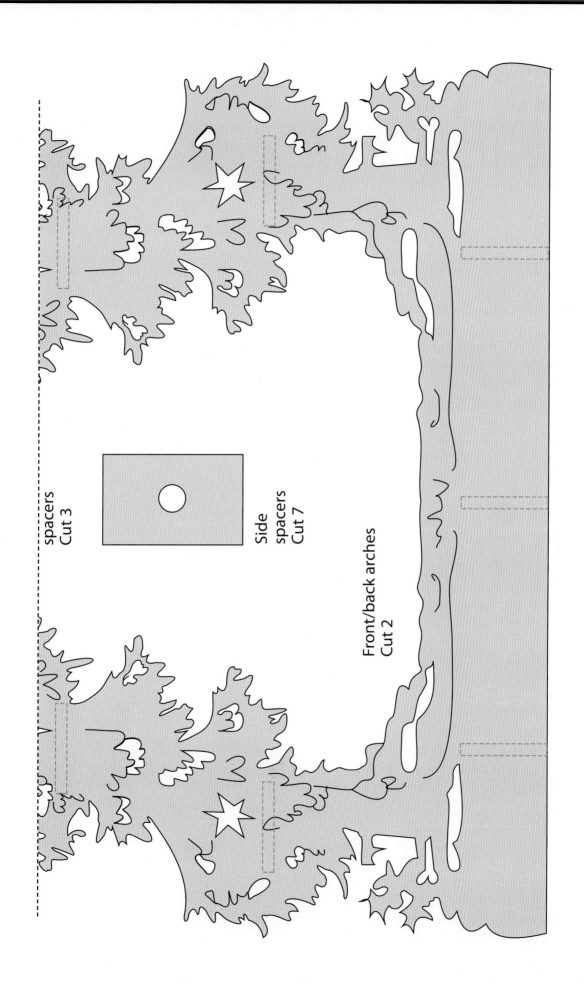

spacers
Cut 3

Side
spacers
Cut 7

Front/back arches
Cut 2

Building a
Nativity Scene
Candle Holder

By Sue Mey

Scenes depicting the birth of Jesus are displayed in various forms of art and are especially popular around Christmas. Nativity scenes are traditionally set in a barn or stable and include Mary, Joseph, baby Jesus, angels, shepherds, and the Three Wise Men.

Place two or three candles in votive holders on the base behind the fretwork to illuminate the design. A piece of semi-transparent acrylic adds color to the scene. Battery-operated candles are available in various shapes and sizes and may be used as a safe alternative to wax candles.

1 Prepare the blanks. Trace the rough shape of the candle holder fretwork onto the blank. Cut along the lines. The smaller blank is easier to maneuver as you cut the fretwork. Cut the base to the dimensions listed in the materials list.

2 Attach the patterns. Cover the candle holder fretwork blank with masking tape. Attach the pattern to the blank with spray adhesive or a glue stick. Stack cut the blanks to create two projects.

3 Drill the blade-entry holes. For the large open areas, use a ⅟₁₆"-diameter bit. For the smaller areas, use a ⅟₃₂"-diameter bit.

4 Cut the frets. For the large areas, use a #3 or #5 reverse-tooth blades. Switch to a #2/0 blade for the smaller areas.

5 Cut around the perimeter of the blanks. Cut or sand up to the perimeter lines. I find it easier to sand the smooth curves of this design rather than cutting them.

6 Assemble the pieces. Remove the tape and patterns. Carefully hand sand the pieces and remove the sanding dust. Glue and clamp the upright to the base using wood glue. Apply a clear spray varnish or your finish of choice. Use epoxy or cyanoacrylate (CA) glue to attach the optional acrylic to the back of the fretwork.

Use transparent acrylic or
omit the backing board for a
distinctly different look.

materials
& tools

Materials:

- ⅜" to ½" x 6¾" x 11¼"
  hardwood or plywood
  (fretwork)
- 6¾" x 10½" semi-
  transparent acrylic
  (optional backing)
- ¾" x 3" x 6½"
  hardwood or plywood
  (base)
- Masking tape
- Temporary-bond spray
  adhesive or glue stick
- Wood glue
- Sandpaper,
  assorted grits
- Clear spray varnish

Tools:

- #2/0 and #3 or #5
  reverse blades or
  blades of choice
- Drill press with ¹⁄₃₂"-
  and ¹⁄₁₆"- diameter bits
- Disc sander (optional)
- Assorted clamps

Holiday Tealight Candle Holder

By Bruce Pratt

Eight silhouette designs let you create dramatically different looks by choosing multiple images or a single design for a holder for a battery-powered tealight. Select the Star of David for a beautiful Hanukkah gift or choose the five-pointed star for a holder than can be displayed year round.

The design is constructed from 12 panels and depends on relatively precise miters on the five edges of each panel. Mathematically, the angle of the miter is 31.72°, but it is best to start with 32° miters and sand them to a precise fit.

You can cut the miters by angling the table on your scroll saw to make the perimeter cuts (method A) or by sanding them to the correct angle with a disc sander (method B). For both methods, pre-sand the blanks with progressively finer grits of sandpaper up to 220 grit. Attach the patterns to the stock, orienting the grain in the same direction on all the pieces.

A1 **METHOD A, STEP 1: Cut the miters.** Tilt either side of your saw table down 32°. Position the pieces on the lower side of the table and cut along the perimeter. Cut three panels to test the miter angle.

A2 **METHOD A, STEP 2: Smooth the edges.** Sand the edges of each panel lightly to remove any rough edges or burrs produced by the cutting. Do not round over the edges.

B1 **METHOD B, STEP 1: Cut out the panels.** Check to make sure your saw table is square to the blade. Cut around the perimeter of all 12 panels. Draw a few pencil lines on the edges of the panels to help guide you during the sanding process.

B2 **METHOD B, STEP 2: Sand the miters on three panels.** Set your disc sander table to 32° or construct a jig to hold the blank at 32° (see sidebar page 105). Sand all five edges of the blank until the pencil line is just barely removed. Do not oversand.

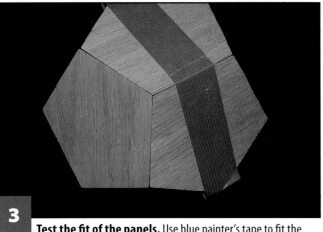

3 **Test the fit of the panels.** Use blue painter's tape to fit the three pieces together. If there is a gap at any of the three edges where the pieces meet, increase the angle at which the scroll saw table or the sander is tilted, adjust the miters, and test the pieces again. Prepare the remaining nine panels.

4 **Cut the fretwork.** Attach fretwork patterns to ten panels. The top of the design should be at the point on five of the panels and opposite the point on the other five panels. Drill ⅛"-diameter blade-entry holes. Cut the fretwork using a #3 reverse-tooth blade. Make sure the scroll saw table is square to the blade.

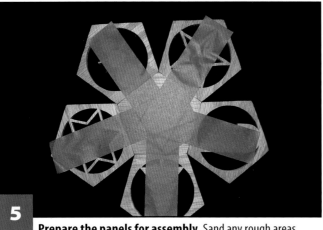

5 **Prepare the panels for assembly.** Sand any rough areas with 220-grit sandpaper. Use the inside of a panel as a guide to cut ten pieces of tracing paper or rice paper. Mask off the miters and apply your finish of choice. I use an oil finish. Allow the finish to dry thoroughly. Arrange the lower sides and base in position with the miters facing down. Apply blue painter's tape as shown.

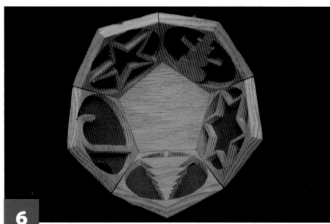

6 **Assemble the holder.** Flip the pieces over, add a minimal amount of glue to the miters, and form a basket shape. Wrap an additional ring of blue painter's tape around the sides. Make sure the edges and corners are correctly aligned. Use tape to hold the other five panels in place as you glue them to the top of the first five panels. Add a dot of glue to each corner of the paper panels and place them in position. Do not glue the lid in place. The lid rests on the top of the sides and can be removed to insert the battery-powered tealight.

materials & tools

Materials:
- 12 each ¼" x 3" x 3" plywood or wood of choice
- Blue painter's tape
- Spray adhesive
- Assorted grits of sandpaper, up to 220 grit
- Tracing paper, rice paper, or translucent paper
- Battery-powered tealight candle
- Wood glue

Tools:
- #3 reverse-tooth blades or blades of choice
- Disc or belt sander
- Drill with ⅛"-diameter drill bit

Alternate Uses

This project can be used as a candy dish with no changes. To use it as an ornament, glue the top panel in place and attach a small brass eye hook to the top. For a completely different effect, omit the paper backing.

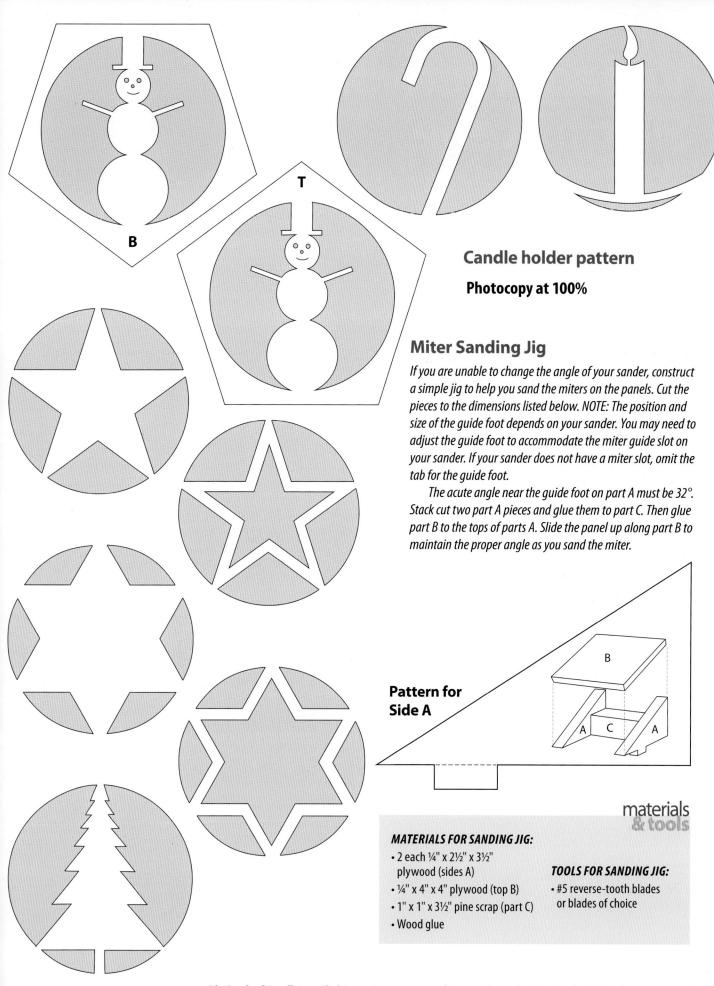

Candle holder pattern

Photocopy at 100%

Miter Sanding Jig

If you are unable to change the angle of your sander, construct a simple jig to help you sand the miters on the panels. Cut the pieces to the dimensions listed below. NOTE: The position and size of the guide foot depends on your sander. You may need to adjust the guide foot to accommodate the miter guide slot on your sander. If your sander does not have a miter slot, omit the tab for the guide foot.

The acute angle near the guide foot on part A must be 32°. Stack cut two part A pieces and glue them to part C. Then glue part B to the tops of parts A. Slide the panel up along part B to maintain the proper angle as you sand the miter.

Pattern for Side A

materials
& tools

MATERIALS FOR SANDING JIG:
- 2 each ¼" x 2½" x 3½" plywood (sides A)
- ¼" x 4" x 4" plywood (top B)
- 1" x 1" x 3½" pine scrap (part C)
- Wood glue

TOOLS FOR SANDING JIG:
- #5 reverse-tooth blades or blades of choice

Vintage Fretwork Sleigh Scene

By John A. Nelson

This fretwork design makes an impressive shadow box portrait, especially when mounted on mirrored acrylic. The project is a great way to showcase your Christmas cards. Tack a ribbon to the back of the holly leaves and attach the cards to the ribbon.

If using hardwood, stack cut the project and align the grain with fragile areas, such as the reins. Apply a coat of Danish oil to seal the hardwood. You can cut the project from Baltic birch plywood and highlight it with acrylic paints. Attach a hanger to the back to complete the project.

Turn the project into a cardholder with a few strands of ribbon.

materials & tools

MATERIALS:

- ¼" to ½" x 7¼" x 14½" cherry or wood of choice
- Assorted grits of sandpaper up to 220 grit
- Danish oil or finish of choice
- Saw-tooth hanger

TOOLS:

- #1 reverse-tooth blades or blades of choice
- Drill with ¹⁄₁₆"-diameter drill bit
- Brushes or rags (to apply finish)

Vintage fretwork sleigh pattern　　　　**Photocopy at 100%**

Nostalgic Sleigh Centerpiece

By John A. Nelson

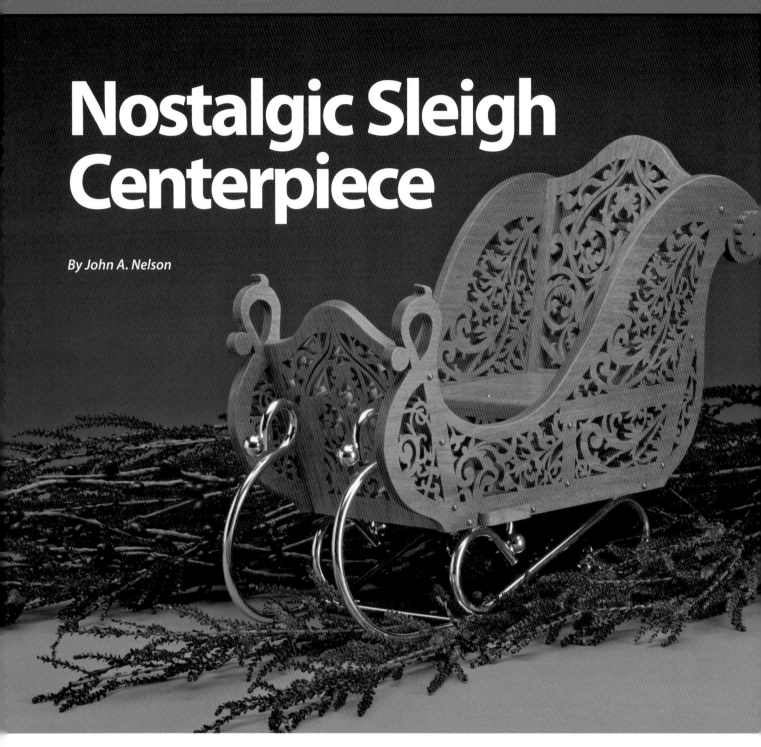

This turn-of-the-century-style sleigh design can be used in a number of ways: Fill it with candy or nuts for an attractive serving dish or surround it with greens for an elegant centerpiece.

The sides can be stack cut, and there are no frets in the seat or bottom, so cutting is easier than it looks. Assembly guides are clearly marked on the pattern. Use the exploded diagram to clarify and assist with final assembly.

While the sleigh is a beautiful project all on its own, it is possible to add a music box mechanism under the seat.

The patterns are sized for ³⁄₁₆"-thick material. I recommend cherry or maple for its beauty and strength. It is possible to substitute ¼"-thick material, but the additional thickness will make it difficult to fit the pre-made sleigh runners.

After cutting and sanding the pieces, attach the sides, front, and back to the base with wood glue. After the glue dries, you can add the optional music box movement.

Support
3/16" thick - cut 1

Sleigh centerpiece pattern

Photocopy at 100%

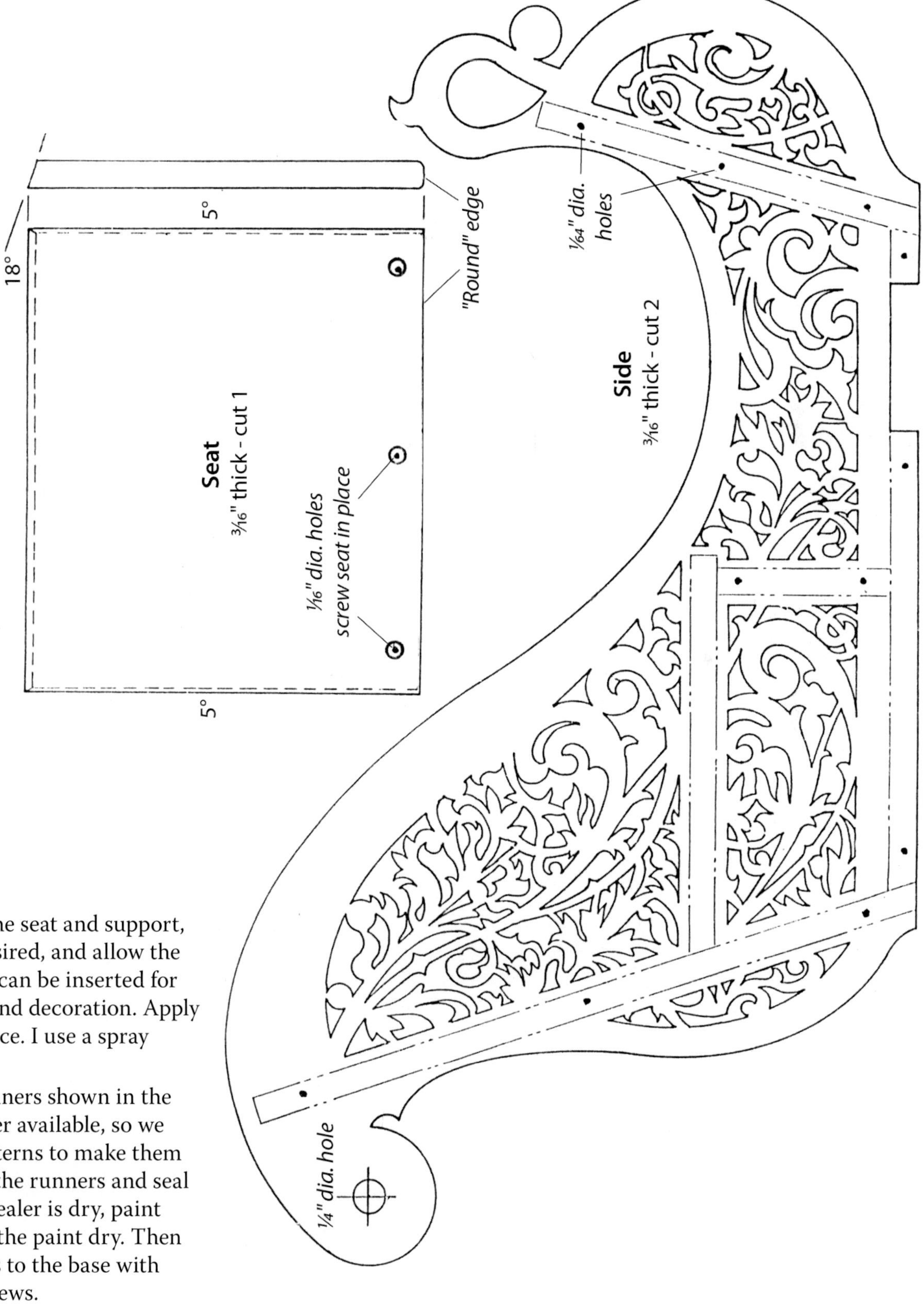

Seat
3/16" thick - cut 1

1/16" dia. holes
screw seat in place

5°

18°

5°

"Round" edge

1/64" dia. holes

Side
3/16" thick - cut 2

1/4" dia. hole

Then attach the seat and support, using screws if desired, and allow the glue to dry. Brads can be inserted for added durability and decoration. Apply your finish of choice. I use a spray lacquer.

The metal runners shown in the photo are no longer available, so we have provided patterns to make them from wood. Sand the runners and seal them. When the sealer is dry, paint them gold and let the paint dry. Then attach the runners to the base with epoxy or small screws.

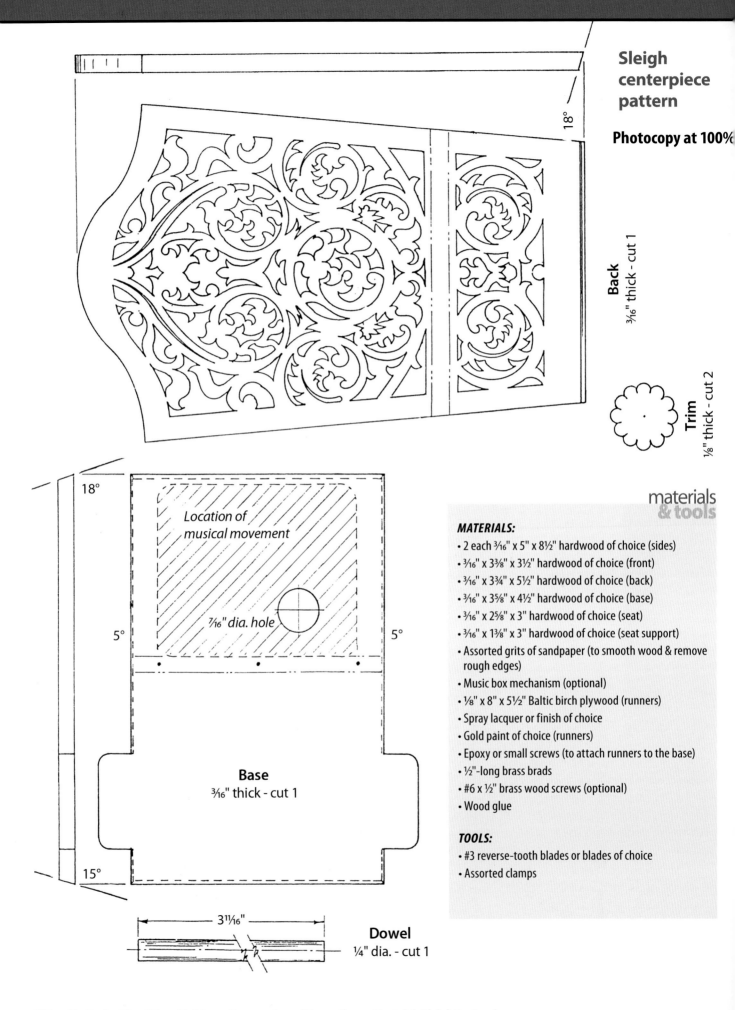

Sleigh centerpiece pattern

Photocopy at 100%

18°

Back
3⁄16" thick - cut 1

Trim
1⁄8" thick - cut 2

18°

5°   5°

Location of musical movement

7⁄16" dia. hole

Base
3⁄16" thick - cut 1

15°

3¹¹⁄₁₆"

Dowel
¼" dia. - cut 1

materials & tools

MATERIALS:

- 2 each 3⁄16" x 5" x 8½" hardwood of choice (sides)
- 3⁄16" x 3⅜" x 3½" hardwood of choice (front)
- 3⁄16" x 3¾" x 5½" hardwood of choice (back)
- 3⁄16" x 3⅝" x 4½" hardwood of choice (base)
- 3⁄16" x 2⅝" x 3" hardwood of choice (seat)
- 3⁄16" x 1⅜" x 3" hardwood of choice (seat support)
- Assorted grits of sandpaper (to smooth wood & remove rough edges)
- Music box mechanism (optional)
- 1⁄8" x 8" x 5½" Baltic birch plywood (runners)
- Spray lacquer or finish of choice
- Gold paint of choice (runners)
- Epoxy or small screws (to attach runners to the base)
- ½"-long brass brads
- #6 x ½" brass wood screws (optional)
- Wood glue

TOOLS:

- #3 reverse-tooth blades or blades of choice
- Assorted clamps

Sleigh centerpiece pattern

Make crosspieces to tie sides together, and mount sleigh. ¼" Baltic Birch ⅜" wide by 2½" long.

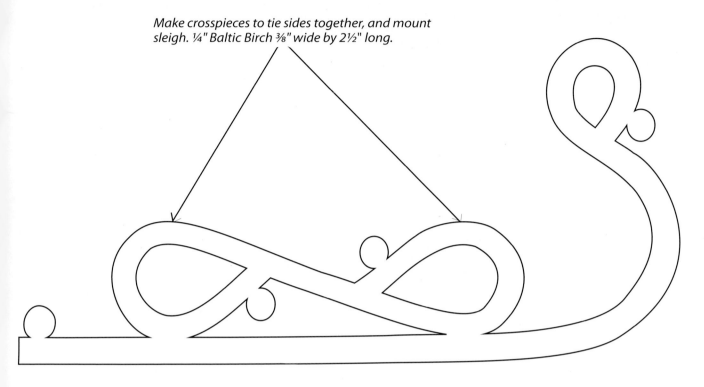

Cut runners from ⅛" Baltic birch. Give them a good coat of sealer (to smooth the surface), then paint gold.

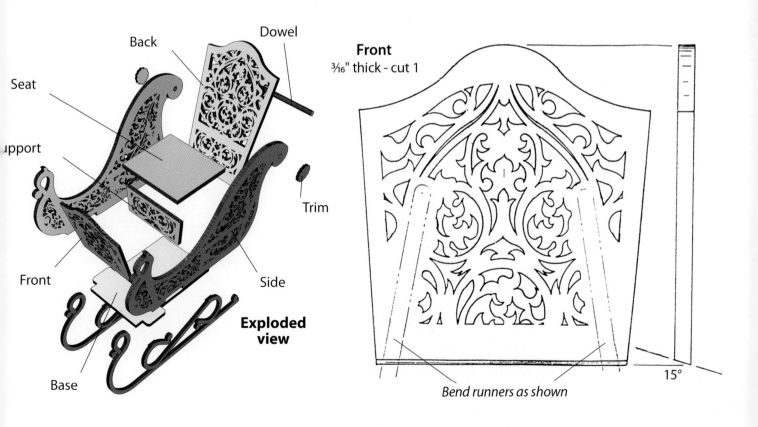

Back

Dowel

Seat

Support

Front

Base

Trim

Side

Exploded view

Front
³⁄₁₆" thick - cut 1

Bend runners as shown

15°

Peace

By John A. Nelson

This exquisite design is inspired by Italian-style letters developed by Luca Pacioli in the late 1400s. The sharp angles and flowing circles create a pleasing harmony.

The pattern can be cut from a variety of materials including hardwood, plywood, thin metal, acrylic, or paper. Cut a colored acrylic backer to create a stunning stained glass effect. Sandwich several sheets of colored paper between thin plywood or cardboard to create overlays for custom Christmas cards.

This pattern is sized for ⅜"-thick material. It can be enlarged or reduced to suit your needs. If you choose to enlarge the pattern, I recommend using thicker wood.

You can cut the small circles by using drill bits of different diameters or, if you don't have drill bits to fit, by drilling undersized holes and using sandpaper wrapped around a dowel to sand them to size. The dowel procedure also smooths out the circles if you choose to cut them on the scroll saw.

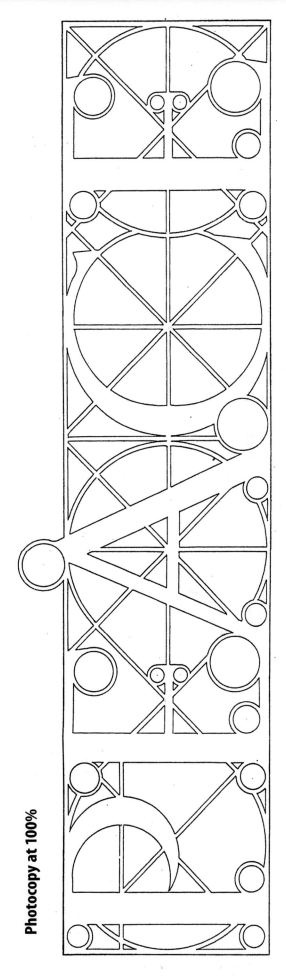

materials
& tools

Materials:

- ⅜" x 3" x 11" hardwood of choice
- Assorted grits of sandpaper
- Dowel (to wrap sandpaper around to sand holes)
- Finish of choice

Tools:

- #5 and #1 reverse-tooth blades or blades of choice
- Drill with assorted sizes of drill bits ranging from ¹⁄₁₆"-diameter through ⅝"-diameter

Classic Santa

By Kevin Daly

This classic image of Santa makes a great holiday decoration. You can turn the portrait into a number of functional projects. You can use the design as a box lid, or add pre-made shaker pegs to turn the design into a custom stocking holder or clever way to display special ornaments.

This pattern is based on a drawing by Thomas Nast. Nast shaped the modern perception of what Santa looks like with his drawings published in the mid to late 1800s.

Stack cut both the mahogany piece and the Baltic birch piece at the same time. Separate the stack, and trim the bottom of the Baltic birch piece so that it fits into a standard 8" x 10" frame. Use a ¼"-diameter Forstner bit to drill the holes for the shaker pegs. Glue the pegs into place.

materials & tools

MATERIALS:
- ⅝" x 8" x 12" mahogany or wood of choice (rack)
- ⅛" x 8" x 12" Baltic birch plywood (portrait)
- 3 each ¼"-diameter shaker pegs
- Frame and/or hanger of choice
- Semi-gloss lacquer or finish of choice
- Sandpaper, assorted grits
- Craft glue
- Black backer board or "Foamie"

TOOLS:
- #5 skip, reverse-tooth blades
- Drill with #59 drill bit and ¼"-diameter Forstner bit

Photocopy at 100%

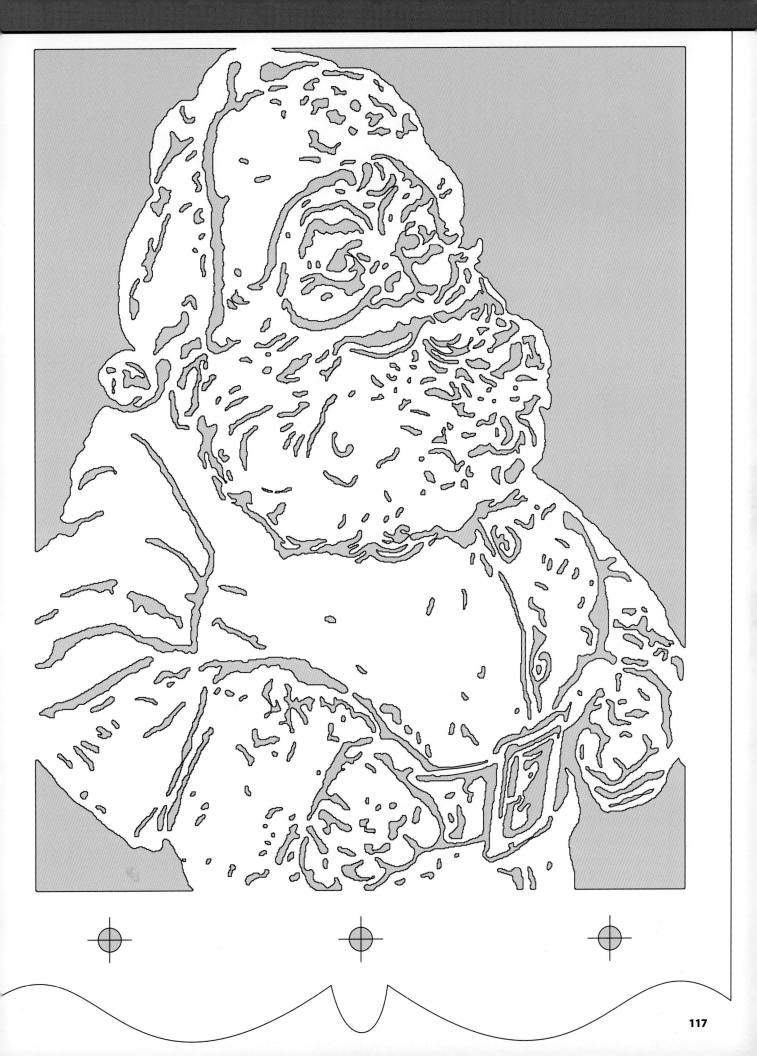

3-D Nativity Display

By Carol and Homer Bishop

This 3-D nativity scene makes a thoughtful holiday gift. The figures are easy to cut and the tabs make assembly a snap.

The sparkling blue nativity is crafted from recycled CDs with a mirrored acrylic base. Use spray adhesive to combine two CDs with the shiny sides facing the outside.

The CDs are stack cut with ¼"-thick lauan plywood for support. Slow down the cutting speed on your saw and use a sharp blade. (Photos and tips for cutting CDs can be found in "Shining Bright" on page 48.)

The stack-cutting method has the additional benefit of producing an identical nativity scene in wood. If you plan to use hardwoods for the project, pay attention to the direction of the grain. For best results, align long slender sections, such as the tree trunks, with the grain of the wood.

Assembling the Nativity

Step 1:   Create the base. Cut the base section from mirrored acrylic. Drill ⁹⁄₆₄"-diameter holes, approximately ⅛" deep for the tabs of the figures. Remove any burrs with a fingernail or craft knife. For the wooden version, the size of the holes for the tabs is based on the thickness of the wood.

Step 2:   Test the fit. If necessary, trim the tabs on the figures with a craft knife until they fit tightly into the holes in the base.

tep 3: Glue the figures to the base. Apply
drop of cyanoacrylate (CA) glue to the tabs
nd glue the figures in place using the photo
a guide.

tep 4: Complete the assembly. Attach the
dditional pieces, such as the tree tops and
p of the manger, using CA glue and CA glue
ccelerator. Lightly sand the wooden pieces
nd round the edges with a flap sander before
sembly. Apply your spray finish of choice to
otect the wood.

**materials
& tools**

MATERIALS:
- CDs or DVDs
- 5 each ¼" x 5½" x 5½" lauan plywood
  (support for figures)
- ¼" x 1¾" x 9¼" lauan plywood
  (base support)
- 1¾" x 9¼" blue mirrored acrylic
  (nativity base)
- Cyanoacrylate glue & accelerator
- Spray sealant, varnish, or finish
  of choice (wood nativity)
- Spray adhesive

TOOLS:
- #4 skip-tooth blades or blades
  of choice
- Flap sander
- Drill press and ⁹⁄₆₄"-diameter bit
- Hobby knife

3-D nativity patterns

Photocopy at 100%

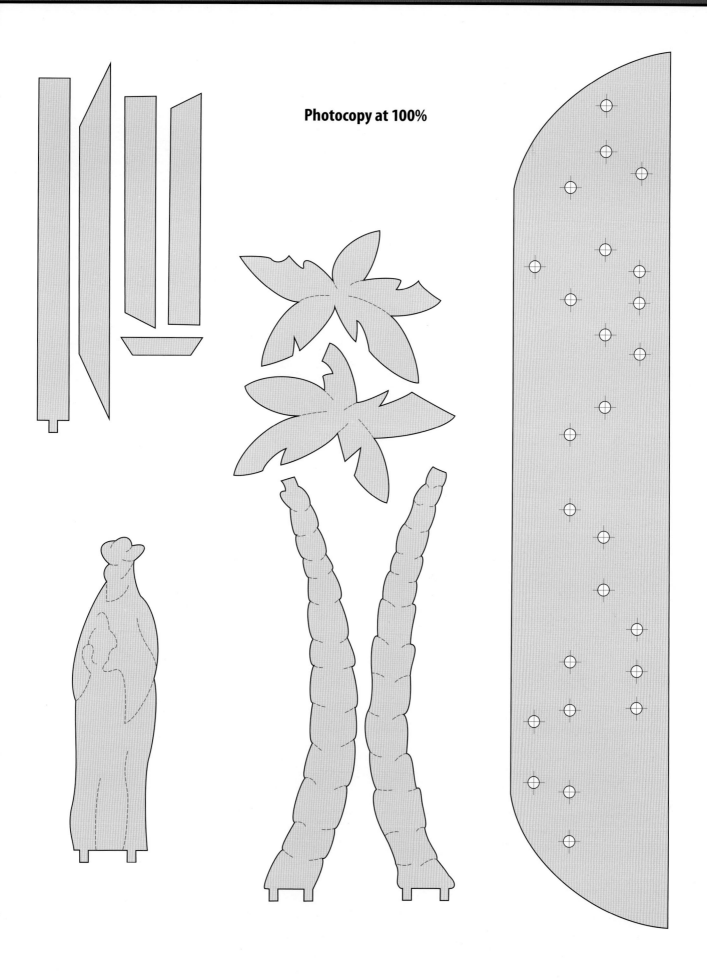

Photocopy at 100%

Christmas Tree Display

1 Transfer the patterns to the blanks. Trace the patterns onto the wood or attach a photocopy using spray adhesive. You will need two copies of the ring pattern. One will be cut on the solid lines, the other on the dashed lines.

2 Cut off the excess wood. Cut around the outside edge of the two octagonal pieces. Use a #5 reverse-tooth blade. This will make it easier to drill the blade-entry holes with a drill press.

By Julie and Fred Byrne

This smart, space-saving Christmas tree is easy to cut and finish. A friend asked us to design a Christmas tree that could be easily assembled for the holiday season and then safely packed away. Made of octagonal rings, a center frame, and an interlocking base section, this tree slides together for an attractive 3-D display, but disassembles easily for flat storage.

The two pieces that make up the center frame fit together with matching slots and are secured on the slotted base. The 12 octagonal rings fit onto the center frame tiers, starting with the largest and then alternating between each set so they overlap slightly as they ascend to the top.

Start by sanding both sides of the Baltic birch plywood with 180-grit sandpaper followed by 220-grit sandpaper. The pieces are easier to sand before they have been cut to shape.

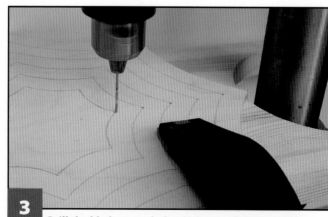

3 Drill the blade-entry holes. Make a small dot just inside the same corner on each of the octagonal pieces. The project looks best if all of the blade-entry holes are made in the same corner of each octagon. Drill 1/16"-diameter blade-entry holes at each of these dots.

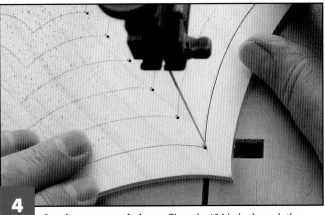

4 **Cut the octagonal pieces.** Thread a #3 blade through the blade-entry holes. Cut each piece so the blade-entry hole is on the inside edge of the octagon. This will make the hole less noticeable when assembled. Number the underside of each piece to make it easier to assemble.

5 **Prepare to stack cut the center frame.** Use masking tape to attach the two blanks for the center frame. Transfer the pattern to the blank by tracing it on using carbon or graphite paper or attaching the paper photocopy with spray adhesive.

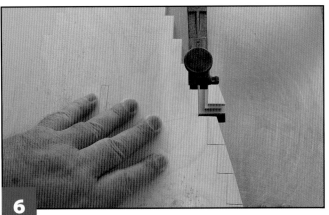

6 **Cut the steps.** Cut horizontally into each step. Then cut in from the other direction to free the waste. Make sure the lines you cut are straight.

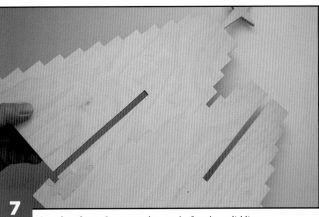

7 **Cut the slots.** Separate the stack. Cut the solid lines on one piece, with the slot starting at the bottom and ending in the center. Attach a second copy of the pattern to the other piece and cut the dashed lines to remove the star and cut a slot from the top down to the center.

8 **Test the fit of the pieces.** Slide the two sections of the center frame together and make sure they fit properly. Then position the octagonal pieces on the tree, starting with the large bottom piece. Slide the slot on the top octagonal piece diagonally over the star on the top of the tree.

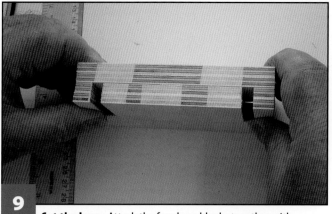

9 **Cut the base.** Attach the four base blanks together with masking tape. Transfer the pattern to the blank and cut the outermost slots on each end. Separate the blanks into two stacks of two, flip one pair, and reassemble the stack. Cut the center slot.

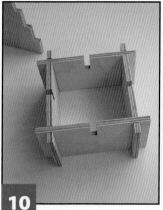

10 **Assemble the base.** Separate the stack. Make sure the center slot faces up on all four pieces. Alternate the pieces so the outside slots fit together. Position the tree in the center slots on the base pieces.

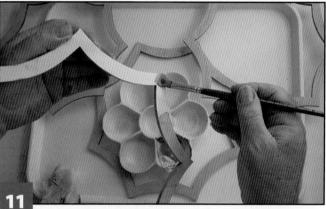

11 **Prepare the pieces for painting.** Hand sand all of the edges with 280-grit sandpaper to remove burrs. Remove the fine dust with a tack cloth. Sort the pieces into groups by the color they will be painted. Paint the octagonal pieces a light green.

12 **Finish the tree.** Paint the center frame pieces a dark hookers green, the base a light brown, and the star silver or yellow. Allow the paint to dry overnight, lightly sand it with 320-grit sandpaper, and wipe it down with a tack cloth. Apply an acrylic matte varnish.

materials & tools

MATERIALS:
- ¼" x 24" x 36" Baltic birch plywood
- Sandpaper, assorted grits between 180 and 320
- Acrylic paint:
Christmas green
Hookers green
Light brown
Silver or yellow
- Carbon or graphite paper (optional)
- Spray adhesive or glue stick (optional)
- Masking tape
- Acrylic matte varnish

TOOLS:
- #3 and #5 blades or blades of choice
- Drill press with ¹⁄₁₆"-diameter (or smaller) drill bit
- Sanding block
- Tack cloth
- Pencil (to trace pattern, optional)
- Ruler (to trace straight lines, optional)
- Paint brushes

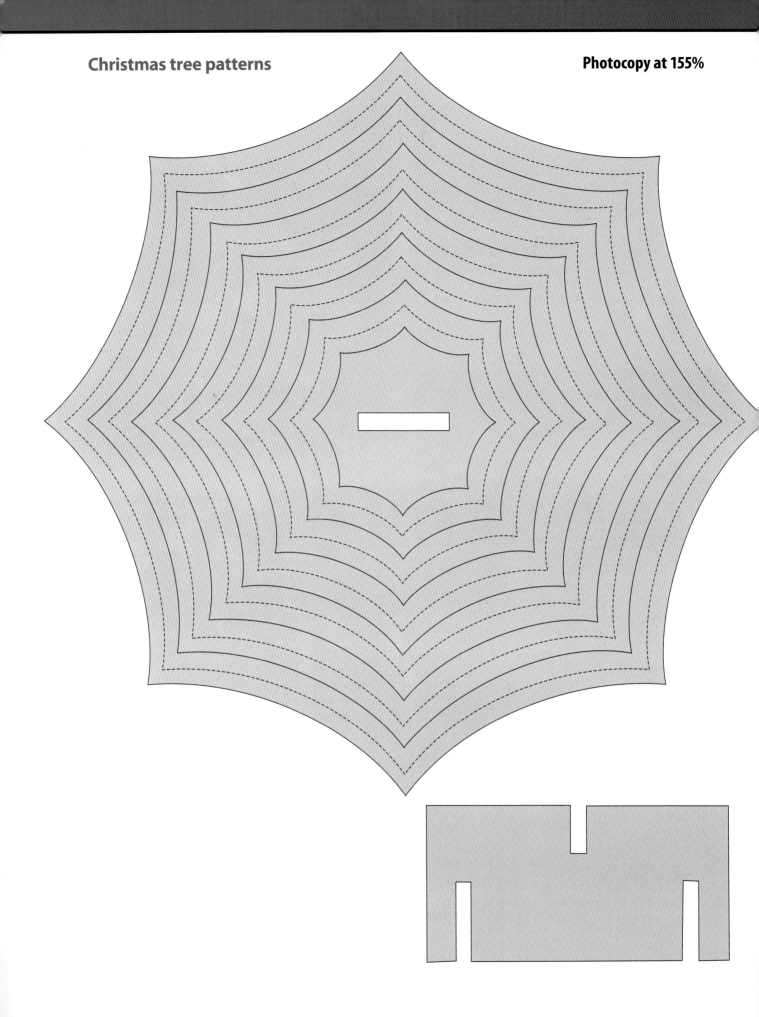

Photocopy at 155%

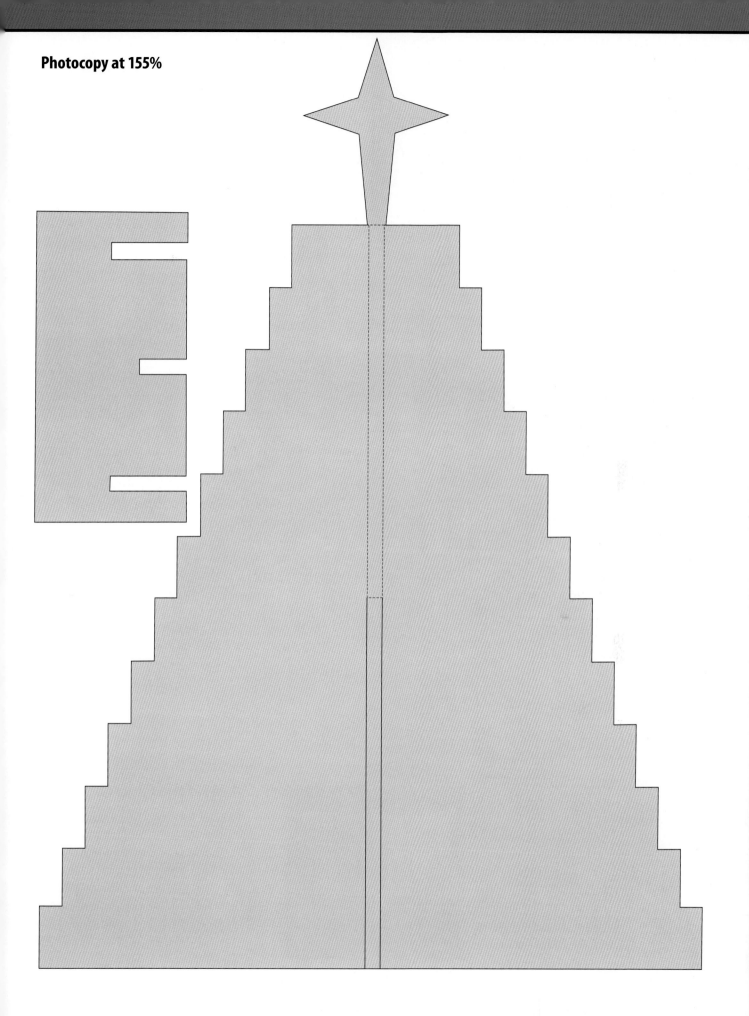

Doves and Cardinals Christmas Tree

by Paul Meisel

This project offers an interesting "twist" on scroll-sawn projects and a new technique for you to try.

A single spiral cut forms the tree. When the birds are added, their weight causes it to uncoil downward, forming the shape of an evergreen tree.

You can use a variety of stains and paints to finish the project to suit your tastes. Don't be afraid to get creative; my original version uses vibrant colors and sparkle glaze, and the ornament picture shows how muted acrylic washes can give it a different look.

I use 10 cardinals and 10 doves, but you can make the project using all cardinals, all doves, or a combination. The slot in the back of each bird allows you to slip it onto the spiral. Do not glue the birds to the spiral. That way, when it is time to put the decoration away, the birds slide off and the tree collapses for easy and compact storage.

The birds also make charming ornaments displayed on their own.

Why doves and cardinals?

Why are these two birds identified with the holiday season? There are various explanations, but these are the most popular: Noah sent a dove out from the ark to look for land. When the dove returned with an olive branch, Noah knew the flood was over. The dove became a symbol of peace. The red feathers of the cardinal are said to represent the blood of Christ.

MATERIALS:

- 2 each ⅛" x 12" x 12" Baltic birch plywood (spiral and bird wings)*
- ¾" x 3½" x 48" pine board (star, bird bodies)
- Temporary-bond spray adhesive*
- Sandpaper, 80 & 120 grits
- Wood sealer
- Carpenter's glue
- Wire, string, or yarn
- Acrylic primer
- Acrylic paints:

White
Opaque red
Christmas green
Metallic gold
Sparkle glaze

TOOLS:

- Olson #443-F, #446-F & #448-F skip-tooth blades*
- Paint brushes
- Drill with ⅛"-diameter bit

SPECIAL SOURCES:
Items marked with an asterisk are available from www.meiselwood-hobby.com, or 800-441-9870.

Step 1: Cut the spiral. Photocopy the pattern, and glue it to your plywood with temporary-bond spray adhesive. The weight of the birds has been calculated to roughly correspond with the stiffness of ⅛"-thick Baltic birch plywood. Cut only the solid black lines on the spiral pattern. The grey dotted lines show where to attach the star and where to place the birds. I use an Olson #443-F blade.

FREEING THE BLADE **tips**

When you get to the end of the spiral, turn off the saw, release the blade from the blade holder, and slip the spiral off the blade. This is faster than backing out along the cut.

Step 2: Cut the wings. The wings are identical for either bird. You can save time by stack cutting four pieces of plywood at a time. I use an Olson #448-F blade.

Step 3: Cut the star from 3/4"-thick pine. I use an Olson #446-F blade. Drill a ⅛"-diameter hole for the wire or string that will be used to hang the project. If you plan to use ribbon or yarn, you may need to drill a larger hole.

Step 4: Cut the bird bodies. Use caution when cutting the slot width in the top and tail sections. The wings are glued in place, so cut that slot just wide enough to allow for the wing and glue. Cut the slot in the tail section slightly wider so the bird will slip onto the spiral after it has been painted.

Step 5: Sand the pieces. Use 80-grit and then 120-grit sandpaper.

▲ Step 6: Assemble the decoration. Glue the star to the center of the spiral as indicated on the pattern. Glue a wing piece in the top slot for each bird body.

▲ Step 7: Paint the decoration. Seal all of the wood parts with wood sealer. Paint the cardinals red with gold beaks. Paint the doves white with gold beaks. Paint the spiral green. Several coats of each color will be required. You will need to stretch the spiral down to get access to the edges for painting. Try hanging the star/spiral assembly from a wire. Then add a weight, such as a spring clamp or a C-clamp, to the outside of the spiral to stretch it out. Top coat all of the painted parts with clear or sparkly finish.

▲ Step 8: Display the project. Hang the project from a string or wire. Pull downward to "uncoil" the spiral, and slip the birds in place. Suggested placement for each bird shown on the pattern is intended only as a starting point. If the spiral does not stretch far enough, reposition some of the birds on the spiral. Adding more birds to the bottom of the spiral will pull the spiral farther down and stretch it out.

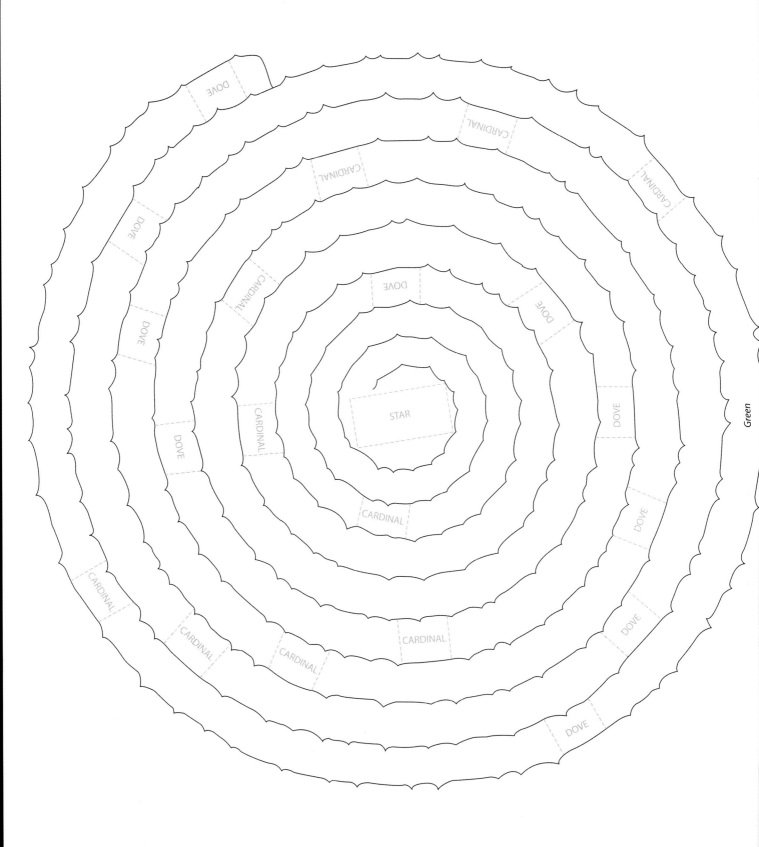

DOVE

CARDINAL

CARDINAL

CARDINAL

DOVE

DOVE

DOVE

CARDINAL

DOVE

DOVE

CARDINAL

STAR

DOVE

CARDINAL

DOVE

CARDINAL

CARDINAL

CARDINAL

DOVE

DOVE

Green

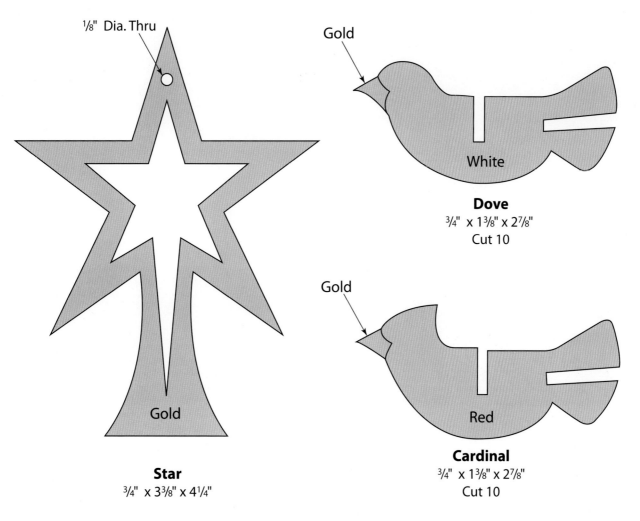

¹⁄₈" Dia. Thru

Gold

Gold

White

Dove
³⁄₄" x 1³⁄₈" x 2⁷⁄₈"
Cut 10

Gold

Red

Cardinal
³⁄₄" x 1³⁄₈" x 2⁷⁄₈"
Cut 10

Gold

Star
³⁄₄" x 3³⁄₈" x 4¹⁄₄"

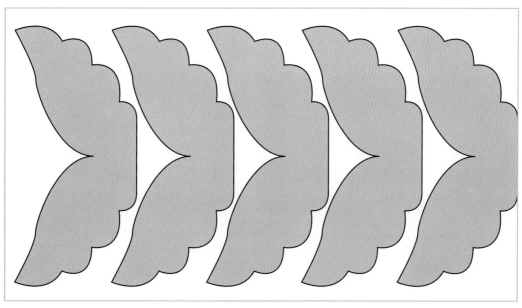

Wings
¹⁄₈" x 3" x 5¹⁄₂" plywood
Stack cut four wings at a time

Christmas Countdown

By Diana Thompson

I designed this advent calendar to count down the days until Christmas with children in mind. I love to watch their excitement grow as each day goes by and Santa gets closer and closer.

I use maple for the base, black walnut for the lettering and numbers, mahogany for the holly leaves, and ½"-diameter wooden balls for the holly berries. When choosing the woods for your project, aim for lots of contrast in color to make each feature stand out.

The calendar can also be painted with craft paints. If you choose to paint your project, use a light-colored wood such as basswood or white pine, so the paint will cover easily.

Start by transferring the patterns to the blanks. I use spray adhesive. Fold the compound-cutting patterns along the dotted line, and align the fold with the corner of the block. Most of the pieces use standard scrolling or compound-cutting techniques, but I've highlighted a few different techniques.

materials & tools

MATERIALS:
- ¾" x 10½" x 6" maple (base)
- ¼" x 4" x 4½" maple (base)
- 2 each ¾" x 1⅜" x 2⅛" mahogany (holly leaves)
- ⅛" x 5¾" x 6½" black walnut (lettering and numbers)
- 2 each 1½" x 1½" x 1½" maple blocks (may glue two ¾"-thick pieces together)
- 6 each ½"-diameter wooden balls
- Spray adhesive
- Double-sided masking tape
- ¾" cellophane tape (to hold the blank together while making the compound cuts)
- Wood glue
- Acetone (optional)
- Sandpaper, 220-grit
- Natural shade Danish oil
- Disposable pie tin
- Lint-free cloth
- Small piece of ¼"-thick scrap wood

TOOLS:
- #3 & #5 reverse-tooth blades, #5 skip-tooth blade, or blades of choice
- Drill and ⅟₁₆"-diameter drill bit
- Disk sander
- Assorted small clamps
- 2 small clamps (optional)
- Ruler
- Small square
- Scissors

1 **Apply three strips of double-sided masking tape to the reverse side of the letter blank.** Remove the backing from the tape and adhere the piece to a small ¼"-thick piece of scrap wood. The lettering is delicate, and the tape and backing piece will keep them from breaking as they are being cut.

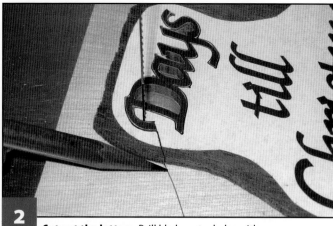

2 **Cut out the letters.** Drill blade-entry holes with a ¹⁄₁₆"-diameter bit. Cut out the frets with a #3 reverse-tooth blade. Enter from the side, cut out the letters, and exit at the point of entry. Keeping the letters confined inside the wood helps to avoid breakage as you cut them out.

3 **Separate the layers.** The tape can be difficult to separate. Turn the letters on their side, and apply a bit of acetone with a small brush. The tape will then release easily. You can also separate the layers with a single-edge razor blade. Use caution so you don't cut yourself or break the letters.

4 **Glue the side pieces to the ends of the tray base.** Then glue the front tray piece in place. Clamp the assembly and allow it to dry. Glue the numbers to the blocks. Glue 0, 1, 2, 3, 4, and 5 on one block and 0, 1, 2, 6, 7, and 8 on the other block. The 6 will be turned upside down for the 9. Center the numbers on each side.

5 **Glue the words to the base.** Use a thin layer of glue so it won't seep out around the edges. Glue the holly leaves into place. Then glue the ½"-diameter wooden balls in the center of each leaf cluster. I left the balls off the right side so you can see the leaf placement more clearly.

6 **Saturate the entire project with Danish oil.** Use a small brush to get inside and around the small areas. I use a disposable pie tin to catch the excess oil. Allow the oil to soak in for 30 minutes. Saturate the project again, and allow it to sit 15 more minutes. Dry off the excess oil with a lint-free cloth, and allow the finish to dry from 8 to 24 hours.

Days till Christmas

⅛"-thick stock

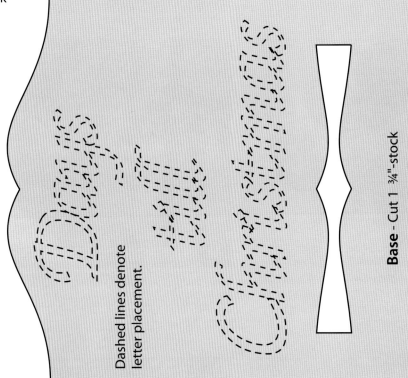

Dashed lines denote letter placement.

Base – Cut 1 ¾"-stock

Photocopy at 100%

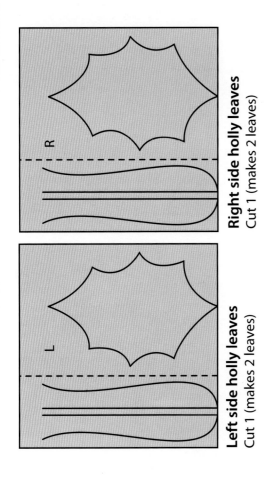

Right side holly leaves
Cut 1 (makes 2 leaves)

R

Left side holly leaves
Cut 1 (makes 2 leaves)

L

Tray front - Cut 1 ¼"-stock

Tray side - Cut 1
¼"-stock

Tray side - Cut 1
¼"-stock

Tray base - Cut 1 ¼"-stock

Numbers for Block 1 ⅛" thick stock

Numbers for Block 2 ⅛" thick stock

Christmas Card Tree

By Sue Mey

Make this festive but simple card holder to display your greeting cards in style.

I scrolled the tree shape from ⅛"-thick MDF. You could also use Baltic birch plywood, or your hardwood of choice. Drill a blade-entry hole in the center of each spiral, and make the cuts with a #2 blade. Sand the cut edges by hand.

You can leave your card tree natural and use a clear finish or add color to the piece. Attach a hanger to the back, or stand the tree up against a wall or other support. Use two fingers to push each spiral from the back and then carefully insert the corner or bottom edge of your greeting card in the opening.

materials & tools

MATERIALS:
- ⅛" x 15" x 19" Baltic birch plywood, MDF, or wood of choice
- Spray paint (optional):
  Dark green
  White
  Red
  Gold (optional)
- Adhesive hanger (optional)
- Assorted grits of sandpaper

TOOLS:
- #2 reverse-tooth blades or blades of choice
- Drill with ¹⁄₁₆"-diameter drill bit

Card tree pattern

Photocopy at 200%

Peace On Earth Plaque

By Paul Meisel

Scroll this timeless message of the holiday season in just an afternoon. The segmentation angel is easy to cut, and when you round over the edges of each segment, it creates a lovely, flowing silhouette.

I cut the letters, angel, and olive branches out of 1/4"-thick maple. Mark the bottom so you don't round over the wrong side. Round over the corners of the angel segments, but don't sand the edges. I use a 1"-diameter drum sander.

The project is mounted on an oval oak plaque. The coarse, open grain of the oak provides a subtle contrast of color and texture with the tight, closed grain of the maple.

These plaques are available in a variety of places, but they are also easy to create on a scroll saw if you have a router equipped with a 3/8"-radius cove and bead bit to shape the edges. Drill a 1/2"-diameter hole in the back of the plaque to provide a space for whatever hanger you use to attach the plaque to the wall.

Use a 1/16"-diameter drill bit to drill blade-entry holes for the inside cuts. Sand any fuzzies from the letters. Place a sheet of clear plastic over the pattern. This lets you assemble the segmentation properly without gluing the pieces to the pattern. Use your glue of choice sparingly; it is difficult to remove any squeeze-out after the pieces are positioned.

Position the segments and the letters on the plaque without applying any glue. When satisfied with the arrangement, remove one piece, add glue to the back sparingly, and replace the piece. Removing only one piece at a time helps retain the placement of the individual pieces. Clamp the pieces in place on the oak plaque with sandbags or a weighted piece of cardboard to dry.

Apply a coat of sanding sealer and sand everything with 220-grit sandpaper. Then apply another coat of sanding sealer or polyurethane. Attach a sawtooth hanger to the back to complete the project.

An alternative would be to paint the angel, olive branches, and letters and leave the plaque with a natural finish.

PARTS IN ORDER
Place your cut segmentation pieces on an extra pattern to keep them organized.

tips

materials & tools

MATERIALS:
• ¼" x 3" x 24" maple or wood of choice (segmentation and letters)*
• ¾" x 9¾" x 16" oak or hardwood of choice (oval plaque)
• Polyurethane sanding sealer*
• Interior satin polyurethane (optional)*
• Paint brushes (to apply finish)*
• Wood glue*
• Assorted grits of sandpaper up to 220 grit*
• Spray adhesive*
• Sawtooth hanger

TOOLS:
• #2 and #5 reverse-skip-tooth scroll saw blades or blades of choice*
• Drill with ¹⁄₁₆" and ½"-diameter drill bit
• Router with ⅜"-radius cove and bead bit (optional)
• Sander of choice (I use a stationary drum or disc sander to smooth out the oval sides of the plaque.)

SPECIAL SOURCES:
Items marked with an asterisk in the Materials & Tools list are available from *www.meiselwoodhobby.com*, or 800-441-9870.

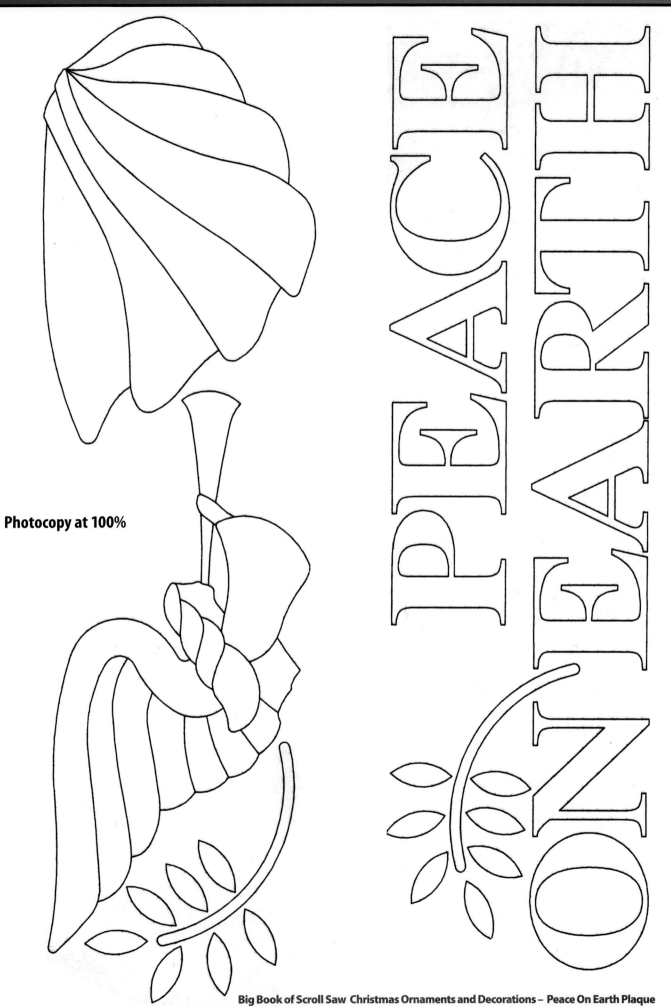

Photocopy at 100%

Peace plaque pattern

½" dia. x ⅜" deep
(back side of plaque)

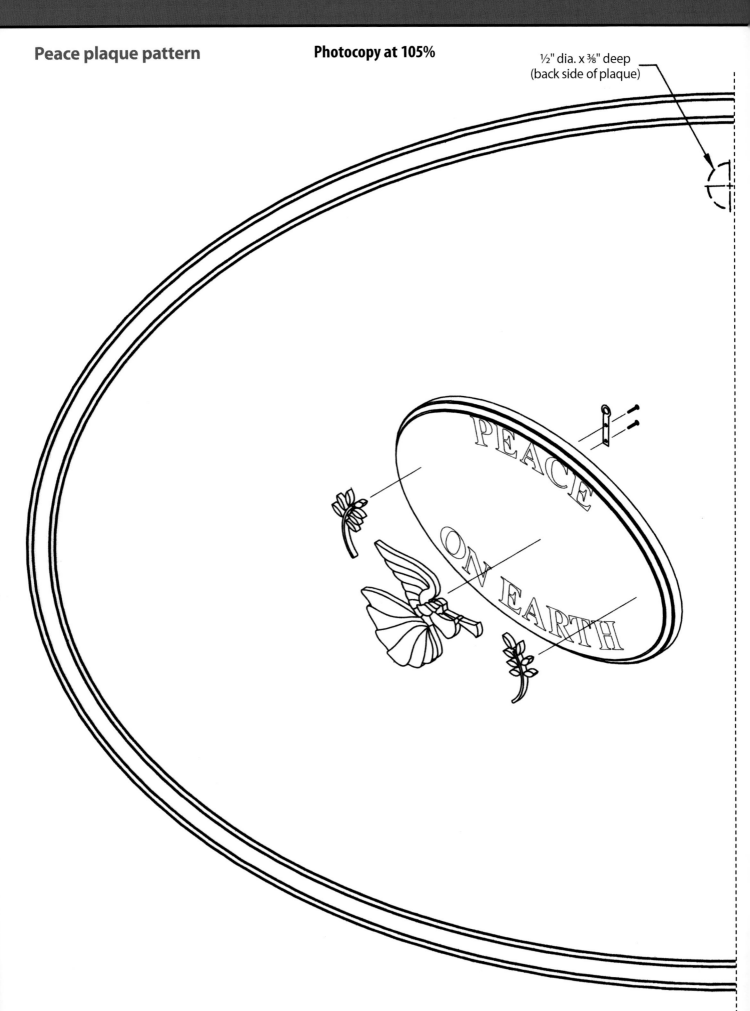

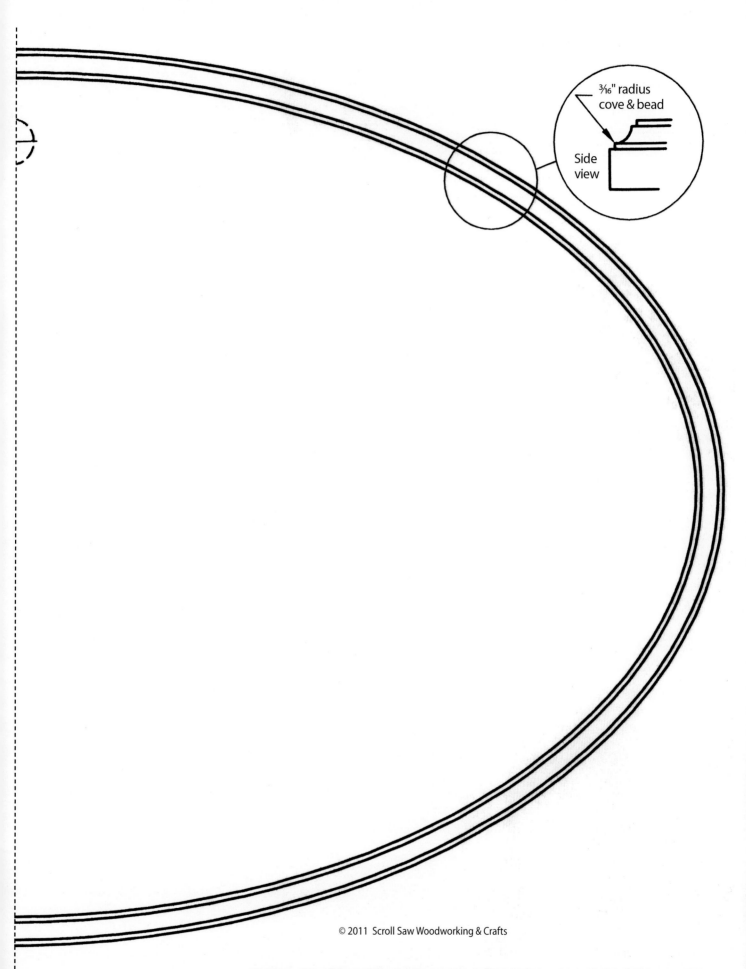

³⁄₁₆" radius
cove & bead

Side
view

Poinsettia Wreath

Varying layers add depth to this intarsia wreath.

By Kathy Wise

Poinsettia flowers signal the beginning of the holiday season more than any other flowers—but a little time in the cold air has them drooping. However, in the form of this intarsia wreath, the poinsettia symbolism will survive almost any weather!

The main part of the wreath is cut from just three pieces of wood: mahogany for the red flowers, black walnut for the leaves, and yellowheart for the center of the poinsettias. You may use any woods of your choice. The varying levels of this piece add to the unique design.

1 **Prepare your patterns.** Make three copies of the pattern. Always keep a master copy to use later. The leaves and flower centers are separated from the main pattern, ready to copy. Cut out the pattern pieces. Tape contact paper flat on a board. Spray adhesive on the pattern and contact paper, and apply the pattern to the contact paper. Cut out each paper pattern piece. Cut out the wreath in four large sections as indicated on the pattern.

2 **Attach the patterns to the work pieces.** Run the grain up and down on all flower sections. The leaf pieces have been separated from the main pattern for easier set-up. Copy and print them as they are laid out. Alternately, separate each leaf and pick your grain direction according to the swirls and knots of your piece of wood, as I did here. Peel and stick the pattern pieces on your selected pieces of wood, lining up the arrow to the grain.

3 **Cut out the pieces.** I use a #5 blade. Make sure your blade is square to the saw table by using an angle to check a cut piece. It is very important to have flat wood for a good cut and fit. Plane any wood that is not flat. Cut out all four large wreath pieces using ¾" thick wood—this will allow you more room to shape your wreath. Cut the dark pieces and the lines with the gray stripes with extra care; they meet the other edges of the wreath pattern. The dotted lines can be left out if you desire, but I think they add a lot to the finished piece. Try to cut out the following pieces first: 6, 13, 16, 24, 28, 29, 41, 46, 45, 58, 60, 64, 69, 75, 72, 86, 88, 90. This will make it easier to cut the remaining pieces. Number each piece on the back with a pencil — certain inks and markers may run and discolor your pieces when you varnish.

4 **Cut out the centers of the flowers.** You can also use a ⅝"-diameter dowel rod and stain it yellow, if you want to skip this step. I used yellowheart for a nice warm yellow color—it was harder to cut, but I think it was worth the effort. Gently round the ends on a pneumatic drum sander. Keep each group of circles together for a better fit by numbering each set.

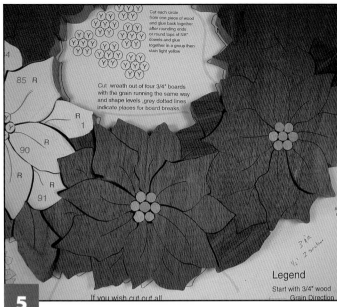

5 **Lay out all the cut pieces.** Place them on a full pattern taped to a work board. Check the fit of the pieces and make adjustments as needed. If you do not like the wood color or grain direction, change it now.

6 **Shape the pieces.** I think this is the most important step in creating a truly outstanding intarsia piece. Rough-in the varying depths by sanding and shaping with a pneumatic sanding drum. Use a pencil to mark the depths on the sides of each piece, and sand down the wood to your line. Work slowly and align each piece in position on the pattern and next to the other pieces to check for fit. Refer to the shaping guide often. Gray-shaded areas are sanded to a lower level. Slightly round all edges on each leaf and flower petal. Start at one end, and work around the wreath. Clean out the cut lines with a hobby knife or carving knife.

7 **Cut the backer board.** Attach a full pattern to the ¼"-thick plywood, and cut ¹⁄₁₆" inside the lines around the entire exterior. Sand the edges on the sanding mop, and stain just the edge.

8 **Apply the finish.** Using a soft rag, hand wipe a natural gel varnish on all pieces, carefully covering the top and all side edges. Let the gel set about 5 minutes, and wipe it off. Let it dry overnight, and put another coat of natural gel varnish on each piece. Let it dry overnight again before gluing. After the pieces have dried, I use a dental tool to gently clean out the cut in the middle of each petal.

9 **Tack sections of the wreath together.** I use 100% silicone glue—this keeps the pieces together while gluing. If you need to take it apart to adjust a piece or two, it will break apart easily. Lay the pieces on the pattern, and tack the petals and leaves together in four or five sections, taking care to follow the pattern closely. Just use one or two tiny drops of silicone per piece. Be careful when putting the two pieces together—you do not want the glue to push up from the seam onto the front of the wreath. Let it dry overnight.

10 **Glue pieces in the tacked sections to your backer board.** Put a coat of wood glue over the entire backer board, and quickly put each tacked section in place. Weight them down with sandbags, working from the outside edges to the inside. Let dry overnight. Trim any overhanging backer board with a rotary tool sanding drum, and touch up the stained edges. I like to put a final wipe of gel varnish on the entire piece at this point. Saturate your wiping rag, and wring it out. Use just a light rub. Don't get a lot on the piece or you will have to spend time cleaning out the cracks. Attach your saw-tooth hanger to finish the project.

materials & tools

MATERIALS:

These are suggested types of wood. You can use your own wood of choice:

- ¾" x 6" x 16" dark walnut
- ¾" x 8" x 48" mahogany
- ¾" x 6" x 6" yellow heart (for the flower centers)
- ¼" x 18" x 18" plywood for the backer board
- Roll of clear contact paper
- Spray adhesive
- 100% silicone glue
- Yellow wood glue
- Natural gel varnish
- Sawtooth hanger
- Wiping rags

TOOLS:

- #3 or #5 reverse-tooth blades or blades of choice
- Pneumatic drum sander

Poinsettia Wreath Patterns

Photocopy at 230%

- Cut wreath out of four ¾" boards with the grain running the same way and shape levels. Gray dotted lines indicate places for board breaks.

- For an easier pattern, cut all the leaves and flowers out of three pieces of wood. Stain the leaves a darker shade instead of cutting them out of darker wood.

- Number all pieces on the back as you cut them. This will make it much easier to place them back onto the pattern for fitting and finishing.

- If you wish, cut out all dotted lines on the holly leaves in the wreath for a more detailed piece. Use the numbers for placement.

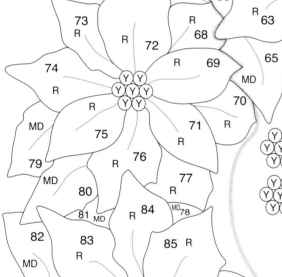

Cut each circle from one piece of wood and glue back together after rounding ends or round tops of ⅝" dowels and glue together in a group then stain light yellow.

Legend
Start with ¾" wood
⟵———— Grain direction
MD...........Medium dark
Y.............Yellow
R.............Deep red

Color Variations

Photocopy at 230%

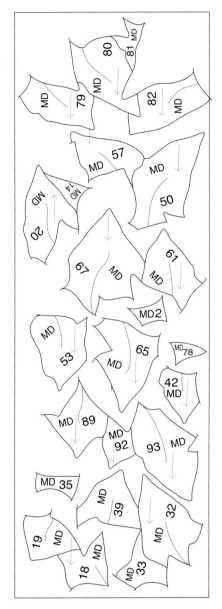

The leaves, which appear in the main pattern, are separated here for easier setup.

Shaping Guide

Crafting a
Christmas Angel Wreath

By Kathy Wise

Greet holiday visitors
by hanging this
heavenly angel on your
front door. The project
also makes a beautiful focal
point hung above your
fireplace mantel.

This wreath is easier to complete
than it looks. Cut the angel from one piece of aspen
and stain the gown and slippers white. You can cut
the pieces from different woods if you prefer. The
wreath is cut from two pieces of cedar and joined in
the middle.

Always keep a master copy of your pattern for
later use. Make six copies of the pattern. Cut the
pattern pieces apart and separate them into color
groups. Tape contact paper flat on a board. Spray
adhesive on the pattern pieces and position them

on the shiny side of the contact paper. Cut the pieces
apart. The contact paper can be re-positioned as
needed and it is easy to remove after cutting.

It is important to start with flat wood for a good
cut and fit. Plane any wood that is not flat before you
lay out your pattern. Make sure your blade is square
to the saw table by using a square to check a cut piece.

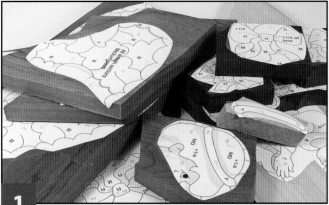

1 **Choose your wood.** Peel and stick the pattern pieces onto your selected pieces of wood. Align the grain direction with the arrows on the pattern. Tape a full-size copy of the pattern to the backing board.

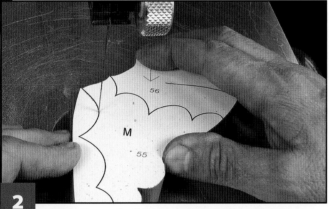

2 **Cut the pieces.** Carefully cut the pieces using a #5 reverse-tooth blade for the aspen and cedar. Use a #5 skip-tooth blade for the harder woods. Number the back of each piece with a pencil. Position the cut pieces on the full-size pattern.

3 **Assemble the eye.** Drill a blade-entry hole and cut the two eyeball pieces from the aspen face. Save the white section. Cut the pupil from a piece of ebony or woodburn the pupil area. Glue the eyeball pieces together and round the section with a drum sander.

4 **Check the fit of the pieces.** Assemble all of the pieces on the pattern taped to the backing board and check for fit. Also check the grain pattern and color of the pieces. If you want to make any color or grain direction changes, do it now.

5 **Cut the risers.** Place the hair, wing, and gown on the riser stock and trace around them. Cut just inside the traced line. Place the risers in position on the pattern taped to the backing board.

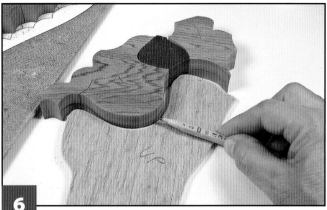

6 **Mark the pieces to sand and shape.** Mark the thickness of the shims on the edges of the pieces adjacent to the shimmed areas. Do not sand below this line or the shim will be exposed. Use the shaping guide to mark the top of individual pieces, indicating the areas to be sanded lower.

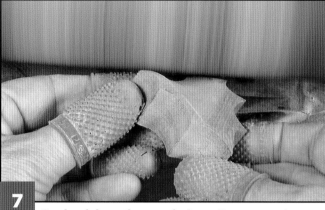

7 **Sand and shape the wreath pieces.** Use a pneumatic drum sander, oscillating spindle sander, and sanding drum, or a rotary power carver with a small sanding drum. Replace the pieces back together often to check the fit and flow. Put a slight concave slope on the middle of the leaves for a realistic look.

PROTECT YOUR FINGERS   **tips**

I wear rubber fingertips, like those found in office supply stores, to protect my fingers while sanding on a big sanding drum. Let it dry overnight. If the grain rises, sand it lightly.

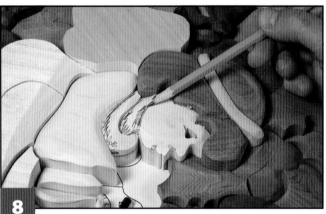

8 **Shape the angel pieces.** Start with the lowest pieces: the back sleeve and the back hand. Mark, sand, and replace each piece to check your progress. I use a hobby knife to carve small areas and add details. You could use a rotary power carver or traditional carving tools.

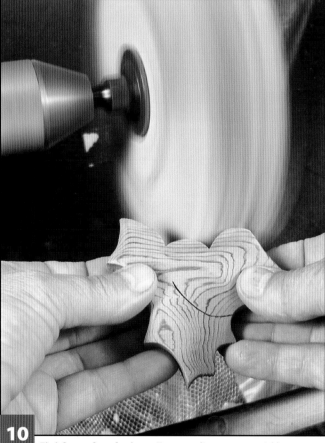

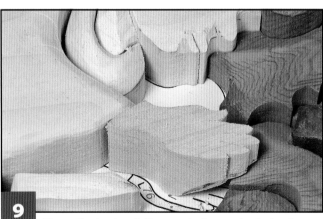

9 **Shape the top hand.** The wreath pieces under the hand should be sanded lower so the hand will fit on top. Place the hand next to the wreath pieces and mark the bottom. Sand the bottom of the hand so it fits over the wreath. Round the top of the hand and carve the areas between the fingers.

10 **Finish sand each piece.** Use a sanding mop to quickly get into all of the curves and crevices, and to add a sheen to the wood. Softer woods such as cedar will sand down quickly, but the harder woods will take a bit longer to sand smooth.

11 **Stain the gown and shoes.** I use a white stain to add contrast between the light aspen of the exposed skin and the white gown and shoes. Follow the manufacturer's directions. Let the stain dry overnight. If the grain rises, you will need to lightly sand with 220-grit sandpaper to remove the rough areas.

12 **Glue the sections together.** Put a few drops of 100% silicone glue/caulk on the edges of the pieces you want to connect. Glue the angel as one section and glue the wreath in several sections. Let the silicone dry overnight. Trace around the wreath onto the backing board. Cut ⅛" inside the traced line. Sand and stain or paint the edges of the backing board.

13 **Glue the intarsia to the backing board.** Assemble the sections on the backing board. Glue the intarsia in place. Only lift one section at a time. Apply wood glue and a few dots of cyanoacrylate (CA) glue to the back of the intarsia. Spray CA glue accelerator on the backing board and replace the section. Use the same technique to glue down all of the sections.

14 **Apply the finish.** I use clear satin spray polyurethane varnish. Let the finish dry and apply a second coat. Then let the finish dry overnight. Paint clear gloss on the eye for a lifelike shine. Attach a mirror-style hanger on the back of the project, but be careful not to drill the hole through to the front of the piece. Remember to sign and date the back of the project.

materials & tools

MATERIALS:

- ¾" x 8" x 41" medium-tone wood, such as cedar (wreath)
- 1" x 8" x 16" white wood, such as poplar (angel)
- 1" x 5" x 5" dark wood, such as black walnut (hair)
- ½" x 1" x 1" ebony (eye)
- 1" x 8" x 12" red wood, such as bloodwood (bows)
- 1" x 2" x 5" yellow wood, such as yellowheart (halo)
- White stain
- Mirror-style hanger
- Clear gloss wood finish (for eye)
- Satin spray polyurethane varnish or finish of choice

TOOLS:

- #5 reverse-tooth and #5 skip-tooth blades or blades of choice
- Drill with ¹⁄₁₆"-diameter drill bit and drill bit sized for hanger
- Sanders of choice (I use pneumatic drum sanders, an oscillating spindle sander, and a rotary power carver equipped with a sanding drum)
- Sanding mop
- Hobby knife or carving tools of choice

PRESERVE THE COLOR OF WHITE WOOD **tips**

Aspen will turn yellow after you apply a finish. Use white stain to keep the nice white color and allow the grain to show. Apply one coat of stain and wipe it off. Let it dry overnight. If the grain rises, sand it lightly.

Angel Christmas Wreath Pattern

Photocopy at 200%

Cut wreath out of four ¾" boards with the grain running the same way. gray dotted lines indicate places for board breaks.

Use risers or thicker wood to bring up ¼".

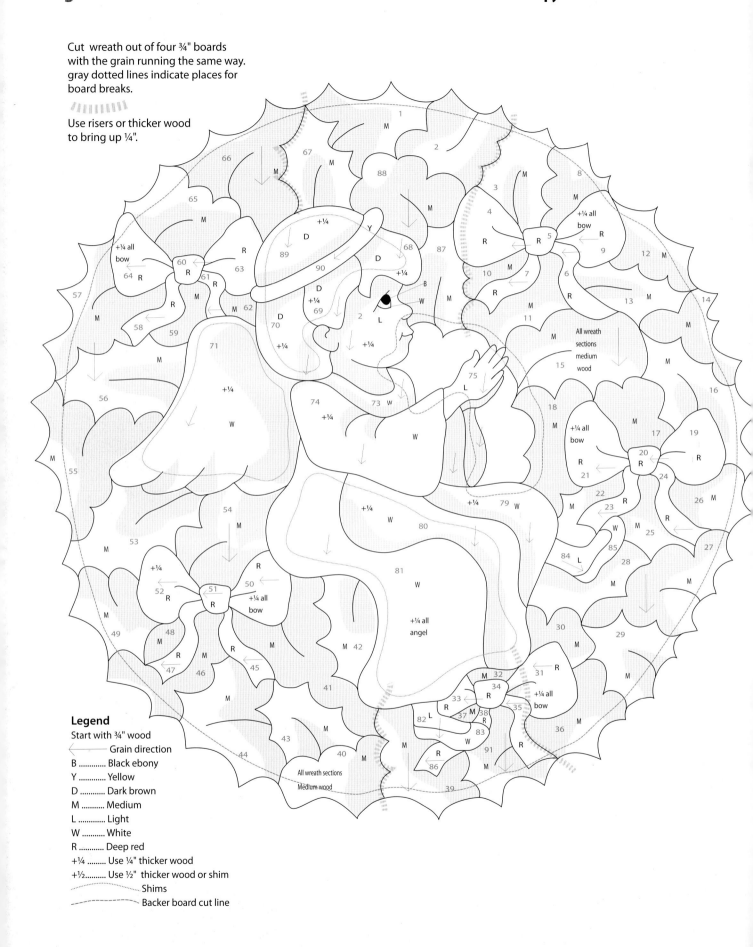

Legend
Start with ¾" wood

⟵ Grain direction

B .... Black ebony

Y .... Yellow

D .... Dark brown

M .... Medium

L .... Light

W .... White

R .... Deep red

+¼ .... Use ¼" thicker wood

+½ .... Use ½" thicker wood or shim

·············· Shims

‒ ‒ ‒ ‒ ‒ Backer board cut line

Season's Greetings Santa

By Judy Gale Roberts

The holiday season typically brings increased visits from family and friends. This cheerful Santa is an ideal way to welcome guests and showcase your woodworking skills. The festive design will outlast many store-bought decorations and is sure to become a family favorite handed down through generations.

The design is relatively simple. To get started, make several copies of the pattern. Make all of the copies at the same time. Copiers can distort images slightly and size variations occur from day to day even when using the same copier.

Santa: Cutting the Pieces

Separate the individual pattern pieces, leaving ⅛" to ¼" of pattern line beyond the part to be cut. This gives you a lead-in line to get your blade on track before you start cutting the part. When the color and grain direction of several parts are the same, cut the parts as a section from one piece of wood.

Note the position of the pattern on the selected wood before applying the adhesive to the pattern. This allows you to easily realign the pattern to make the best use of the wood's color and figure. Make sure your saw table is square to the blade and cut the pieces.

I use 1½"-thick wood for the boots so the toe portion extends far enough to allow Santa to stand on his own two feet. The boots are all cut from the same piece of wood and then the upper portion of the boots are sanded down to ¾" thick. I use a #5 blade for ¾"-thick wood, but use a smaller blade, such as a #1, #0, or #2/0, to make the internal cuts on sections cut from the same piece of wood. Keep the blade in the center of the pattern line. You will need to drill blade-entry holes to cut the fretwork letters on the sign.

Number the back of each piece to keep them in order and keep track of which is the front of the piece. Check the fit of the pieces. If the parts don't fit together properly, you can often see where the pattern line is heavy. Recut these areas with a sharp blade for best results. Sanding pieces to fit usually results in noticeable gaps.

Assemble all of the cut pieces on a master copy of the pattern. I use ¼"-thick plywood to raise the nose, mustache, and lower lip as one section, and another piece of plywood to raise Santa's right glove.

Santa: Shaping and Finishing the Project

Rough in the entire project to achieve the overall depth of the pieces before fine-tuning the parts. After sanding sections, use a pencil to mark the height on adjoining parts. The dotted lines with arrows indicate the contours of individual pieces. The dashed lines indicate wrinkles and grooves, which are added with a Wonder Wheel or rotary power carver. Hand sand the grooves to soften the sharp corners.

Hand sand all of the pieces to remove any cross-grain scratches or pencil marks. Blow off the dust and check for more scratches. Apply a heavy coat of gel polyurethane to the surface and sides of each piece. Let the gel soak for a minute and wipe off the excess. Let the first coat dry overnight and then apply two more lighter coats six to eight hours apart.

When the finish is dry, cut the backing board. Apply a light coat of spray adhesive to a large piece of paper and assemble the pieces on the paper. The adhesive keeps the pieces from sliding around as you trace around them with a pencil. Attach the traced pattern to a piece of hardboard or Baltic birch plywood and cut ¹⁄₁₆" inside the lines. Remove the paper and glue the pieces to the backing board with wood glue.

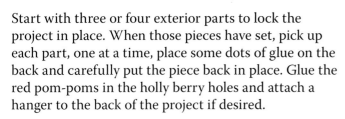

Start with three or four exterior parts to lock the project in place. When those pieces have set, pick up each part, one at a time, place some dots of glue on the back and carefully put the piece back in place. Glue the red pom-poms in the holly berry holes and attach a hanger to the back of the project if desired.

A matching Mrs. Claus pattern is available at www.intarsia.com.

materials & tools

MATERIALS:

- 5 photocopies of the pattern
- Glue stick, spray adhesive, or sticker-making machine
- 1½" x 4" x 6" dark wood, such as dark western red cedar or walnut (boots)
- ¾" x 4" x 4" dark wood, such as dark western red cedar or walnut
- ¾" x 6" x 6" medium-dark wood, such as western red cedar, mahogany, or cherry
- ¾" x 8" x 12" medium-tone wood, such as western red cedar, pecan, or red oak
- ¾" x 5" x 12" light wood, such as western red cedar, oak, or northern white cedar
- ¾" x 6" x 16" white wood, such as aspen, white pine, or holly
- ¼"-diameter by 6"-long dark wood dowels (eyes)

- Polyurethane gel or finish of choice
- ⅛" to ¼" x 14" x 22" hardboard or Baltic birch plywood (backing board and shims)
- Wood glue
- Small red pom-poms (optional)
- Assorted grits of sandpaper

TOOLS:

- #5 and #1 skip-tooth blades or blades of choice
- Sanders of choice
- Rotary power carver or Wonder Wheel
- Drill with ¼"- and ¹¹⁄₆₄"-diameter bits
- Pencil

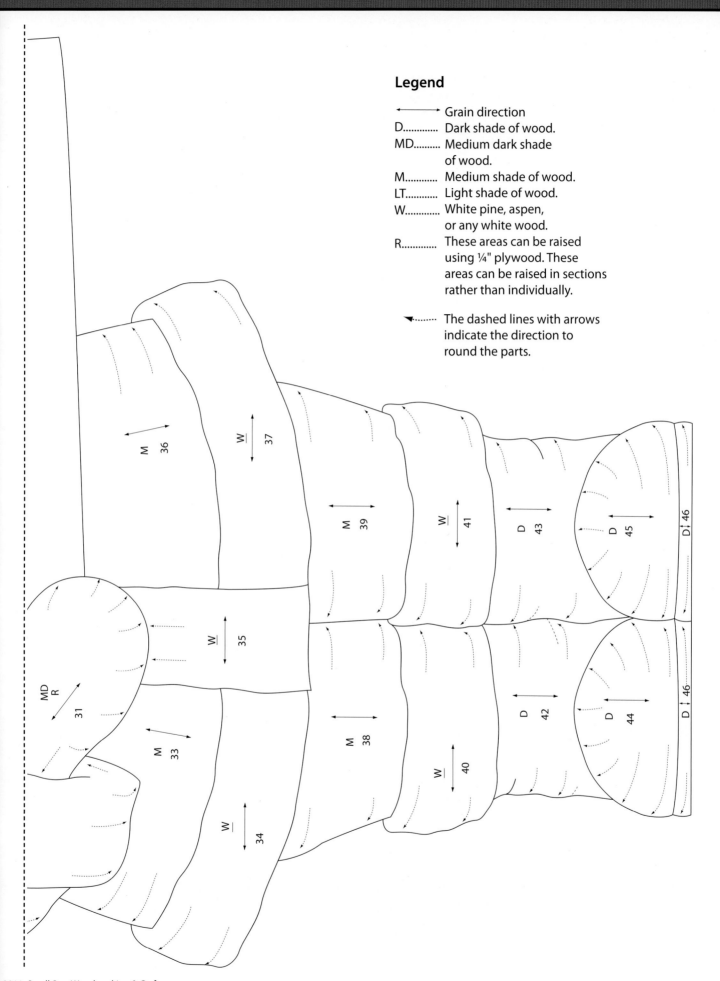

Legend

→ Grain direction

D............ Dark shade of wood.

MD......... Medium dark shade of wood.

M............ Medium shade of wood.

LT........... Light shade of wood.

W............ White pine, aspen, or any white wood.

R............. These areas can be raised using ¼" plywood. These areas can be raised in sections rather than individually.

◄········ The dashed lines with arrows indicate the direction to round the parts.

Contributors

Volker Arnold
Volker, of Germany, designs scroll saw patterns.
www.va-holzkunst.de

Carol and Homer Bishop
Carol and Homer, of Illinois, enjoy cutting and designing intarsia patterns for the following sites. For an e-catalog of their patterns, e-mail *bishoppatterns@yahoo.com*.
www.scrollerltd.com
www.woodenteddybearonline.com

Fred and Julie Byrne
Fred and Julie, of England, enjoy woodworking together and have written a book.
www.picturesinwood.co.uk

Kevin Daly
Kevin, of Connecticut, operates K&J Woodworks.
www.scrollsawpatternsonline.com

Theresa Ekdom
Theresa lives in northern Michigan.
www.woodngoods.blogspot.com

Lora S. Irish
Lora, of Maryland, writes *Woodcarving Illustrated's* Relief Column and has written numerous woodworking and craft books for Fox Chapel.
www.carvingpatterns.com

Gary MacKay
Gary lives in Myrtle Beach, South Carolina, and enjoys gardening and golf.

Paul Meisel
Paul, of Minnesota, is an avid woodworker and designer.
http://www.meiselwoodhobby.com

Sue Mey
Sue lives in Pretoria, South Africa. Her work includes a variety of patterns, special offers, and pattern-making tutorials.
suem@storage.co.za
www.scrollsawartist.com

Stephen Miklos
Stephen, of Connecticut, teaches scrollsawing and lutherie at the Woodworker's Club in Norwalk. *www.carrotcreek.com*

Brad Needham
Brad, of Oregon, describes himself as co-president of the mythical land Needhamia.
www.needhamia.com

John A. Nelson
John, a prolific scroller and designer, lives in New Hampshire.
www.scrollsawer.com

Bruce Pratt
Bruce, of Massachusetts, works in biotechnology and is an avid collector and designer of Gothic window tracery.
designs001@comcast.net

Lynn Reno
Lynn, of Arizona, is a self-taught painter who also enjoys being outdoors.
l.reno2@cox.net

Judy Gale Roberts
The author of numerous intarsia books, Judy has long been recognized as the leading authority on intarsia and was one of the first ten people to be inducted into the Woodworking Hall of Fame.
www.intarsia.com

Tom Sevy
Tom, of Utah, first encountered a scroll saw more than fifty years ago and still finds it relaxing.
www.woodyoubelieveshop.com

Diana Thompson
Diana, of Alabama, is a prolific scroller and designer who specializes in compound cutting.
www.scrollsawinspirations.com

Kathy Wise
Kathy, of Michigan, is a well-known sculptor and intarsia designer with more than 38 articles, 480 intarsia patterns and two books to her credit.
www.kathywise.com
kathywise@bignet.net

Tom Zieg
Tom, of Nebraska, loves to share his knowledge of woodworking with others.
www.woodworkertom.com

Index

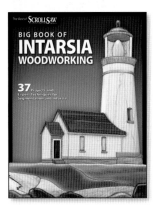
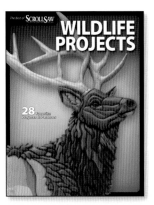

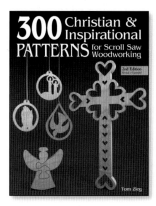